James Branch
CABELL

a reference guide

A Reference Publication in Literature

Jack Salzman
Editor

James Branch CABELL

a reference guide

MAURICE DUKE

G.K.HALL &CO.

70 LINCOLN STREET, BOSTON, MASS.

Library of Congress Cataloging in Publication Data
Duke, Maurice.
James Branch Cabell : a reference guide.

(A Reference publication in literature)
Includes index.
1. Cabell, James Branch, 1879-1958 — Bibliography. I. Series
Z8139.7.D84 [PS3505.A153] 016.813'5'2 78-25985
ISBN 0-8161-7838-0

This publication is printed on permanent/durable acid-free paper
MANUFACTURED IN THE UNITED STATES OF AMERICA

Contents

Introduction

The literary history of every country is filled with the names of obscure writers whose works are known only to the specialist. They are the people whose books, for one reason or another, either did not survive the test of time or else lie untouched on library shelves waiting for the propitious moment when they will be rediscovered and circulated anew. Such is the case with James Branch Cabell, an author who in his heyday had no peer, but one whose works now remain largely unknown and unread. The author of fifty-two volumes, eighteen of which form the Storisende Edition, or the Biography of Manuel, Cabell enjoyed enormous but only momentary fame with the publication of _Jurgen_ in 1919. Today most of his books are out of print, and although his plan and dramatic vision were large, his reading public remains small.

Until the publication of _Jurgen_, Cabell attracted only minor attention from the reviewers and none at all to speak of from the critics. Writing ironic romances for a turn-of-the-century generation of readers whose tastes centered on such writers as John Fox, Jr., Kate Douglas Wiggin, and Francis Marion Crawford, to name but three of the more popular ones, he was dismissed as being "all very pretty and very inconsequential," as one anonymous reviewer aptly wrote in 1901. However, as Cabell reached the end of his apprenticeship years, which occurred when _Jurgen_ was seized by the censors in 1920, his reputation fared considerably better. His publisher afforded him the prestige and profit of bringing out his former works collected in a handsome eighteen-volume set, called the Storisende Edition; moreover, the reviewers, led by the efforts of Chicago _Tribune_ book critic Burton Rascoe, began to take notice of him. At first his name and the titles of his books began appearing in the nation's newspapers, such as the Chicago _Tribune_, for which Rascoe wrote, then in the New York and Boston papers, which represented the views of the American literary establishment. It was not long before the name Cabell, which rhymes with "rabble," the author once wryly remarked, became a household word. Literally hundreds of short reviews and notices of him and his works--more than would fill a book twice this size--appeared around the country. He was the subject of lavish praise, many critics and reviewers flatly stating that his literary immortality was assured. His erudition became the center of fashionable bookish gossip, and he was even the subject of the comic strips, indicating how widely known he had become.

Despite his overnight success, however, Cabell still had his band of detractors. Foremost among them were the moralists, those who saw the thinly veiled sexual references in his novels--particularly Jurgen--as bordering on if not reaching into the realm of the pornographic. In addition there were those who found his highly mannered prose style offensive. Finally, and by far more serious, were those who charged Cabell with a lack of seriousness in his novels. It was one thing, they argued, for the general reader to accept a disillusioned fictional hero, but it was entirely another matter for that reader to feel rapport with characters whose veracity was suspect and whose creator held his readers at arm's length.

Cabell's reputation began its downward trend with the national change of mood that ushered in the 1930s. During that decade, which witnessed economic turmoil, a marked rise in socialism, and the coming of World War II, the nation's literati were in no mood for Cabell's finely wrought fantasies set in a mythological realm which seemed to bear little resemblance to the world of reality. Few readers of that decade realized that Cabell was not the risqué writer that the popular media had made him out to be; fewer still realized that rather than writing fantasies of romantic escape, he was actually attempting to answer universal moral questions. Additionally, few readers were able to penetrate the ornate form of Cabell's romances in order to discover the content that lay beneath it. Had they done so, they would have discovered a writer much different from the one they thought lay hidden there.

Although Cabell continued to publish until the mid 1950s, he was destined never to be the writer that the enthusiastic critics and reviewers of the '20s had projected him as being. Unlike many of his contemporaries, he only modestly attracted the attention of the serious critics, as opposed to the popular reviewers. The result was that his works never became a part of the national literary trust, as have those of many of his contemporaries. Again and again, the articles on Cabell tend to be general appraisals of his whole literary canon rather than in-depth criticisms of his specific ideas, techniques, moral vision, and verbal executions. These latter kinds of criticism establish a writer in the literary parthenon of his society. Without them he remains, as has Cabell, an outsider, one waiting in the wings for a call to a fame that may or may not come.

Since the 1950s there have been many calls for a Cabell "revival," and toward the end of the '60s it indeed seemed likely that such a revival was underway. During those years, and on into the '70s as well, there was a flurry of critical activity centering on Cabell. A handful of scholars began publishing critical and biographical articles on him, and two magazines, Kalki and The Cabellian, were devoted entirely to his life and works. Their pages open to scholars and fans alike, these two journals offered those interested in Cabell valuable collections of information. Unfortunately, The Cabellian was allowed to die, but Kalki continues to publish short articles about Cabell, although it lost one of its ablest contributors when James Blish, the noted science fiction writer, editor, and Cabell scholar, died recently.

Because of the enormity of published material on Cabell, much of it consisting of short repetitive newspaper reviews and news notes, I have been forced to be selective in presenting the material in this book. Anyone interested in the complete assemblages of these materials should consult Cabell's personal scrapbooks, which are housed in the Alderman Library at the University of Virginia in Charlottesville and the Special Collections room at Virginia Commonwealth University, in Richmond. In addition to being a novelist, Cabell was also a scholar and bibliographer of his own works. He subscribed to clipping services from the outset of his career, and he meticulously, one might say lovingly, preserved every scrap of published material about himself and his books. These materials may be consulted in their entirety in the personal scrapbooks.

In collecting and annotating the present materials, I have relied heavily on earlier published bibliographies, notably those of Guy Holt, I. R. Brussell, Frances Joan Brewer, and James Hall. I have attempted to check the cumulative accuracy of these works, using them as the backbone for the present work. Additionally, I have drawn hundreds of items from the scrapbooks, but have included, with some minor exceptions, only the most significant materials. Accordingly, I have included reviews from selected newspapers, only those which set the tenor for the nationwide acceptance or rejection of Cabell's books. Therefore, most of the reviews listed here are from the newspapers in Boston, New York, and Chicago. Those from the Baltimore papers, often instigated by H. L. Mencken, and from Richmond, Cabell's home town, also appear. Occasionally some fugitive items, which help us to understand Cabell better, also appear.

Because Cabell has attracted so little attention from the scholarly community, one finds in the pages of this guide a dearth of in-depth critical articles. I would hope that I have been successful in collecting the major ones, although there are doubtless some that have eluded me. Regarding the two journals devoted entirely to Cabell--The Cabellian and Kalki--I have attempted to extract only those articles that would give interested readers some aid in understanding either the man or his works. Anyone concerned with a thorough study of the author might wish to read the entire press runs of both journals. Because Cabell has also been the subject of numerous general appraisals, many of the annotations on individual articles bear a marked similarity, as the reader will note. For many years those writing about Cabell seemed compelled to explain him to their readers in a general way, their attitudes seemingly being that if the reader would only sample his works he would find Cabell worthwhile.

Introduction

I owe a debt of gratitude to many people who have given valuable assistance in the gathering of the materials included in this book. My colleagues at Virginia Commonwealth University, M. Thomas Inge, George C. Longest, Vesta Gordon, and Ray O. Hummel, Jr., have all given advice and assistance, as has William S. Simpson, Jr. of the Richmond Public Library. The staff of both the Manuscripts Room in Alderman Library and the newspaper archives section of the Library of Congress have aided me in locating and using materials, as has the staff of the Virginia State Library, in Richmond. Elizabeth F. Duke, my wife and colleague, has shared in the various tasks of collecting, annotating, and arranging this material.

In many ways the existence of this book is owing as much to the Interlibrary Loan staff of the James Branch Cabell Library of Virginia Commonwealth University as it is to me. There is no way I shall be able to repay the excellent professional service afforded me by Jane Westenberger, Eileen Meagher, and Janet R. Howell. Mary White also gave valuable assistance in the formative stages of this project.

Writings about James Branch Cabell

1904 A BOOKS--NONE

1904 B SHORTER WRITINGS

1 ANON. "Under the Shadow of a Fortune." New York Times Saturday Review of Books (5 November), p. 750.
Plot summary of The Eagle's Shadow.

2 ANON. Review of The Eagle's Shadow. The Independent, 57 (10 November), 1095.
The book "portrays all of the weaknesses of human nature subjected one way or another to the influence of great wealth, and then kindly covers them with shining excuses."

3 ANON. Review of The Eagle's Shadow. The Dial, 37 (16 November), 314.
The book is a "rather flippant story of a fortune and its successive possessors."

4 ANON. Review of The Eagle's Shadow. Critic, 45 (December), 576.
The book is "all very pretty and very inconsequential."

5 ANON. Review of The Eagle's Shadow. Athenaeum (17 December), 838.
In this book, Cabell's attempts at elegance are often awkward, and on the whole, "The atmosphere is distinctly American."

6 HOWLAND, GEORGE C. Review of The Eagle's Shadow. Chicago Daily Tribune (12 November), p. 7.
After summarizing the plot, the reviewer finds that the book "belongs to the class known as summer fiction, but it is equally good for winter weather...."

7 ROGERS, E. R. Review of The Eagle's Shadow. Baltimore Sun (30 November), p. 8.

The book is too much in the fashionable mode of the day and it is "rather an overgrown short story than an artistically developed book."

1905 A BOOKS--NONE

1905 B SHORTER WRITINGS

1 ANON. "The Latest Books." Richmond Times-Dispatch (7 October), p. 6.
The Line of Love "must add greatly to Cabell's reputation as a Virginia novelist of force and power."

2 ANON. Review of The Line of Love. The Watchman (12 October), p. 17.
After briefly stating the plot, the reviewer praises the straightforward nature of the love stories, which he assumes to be translations from the original.

3 ANON. "Books of the Day." Richmond Leader (14 October), p. 9.
After briefly stating the plot, the reviewer finds that the stories in The Line of Love are characteristic of their author.

4 ANON. "Books and Bookmen." New York Press (28 October), p. 7.
The Line of Love is a book that has a praiseworthy theme as its central idea.

5 ANON. Review of The Line of Love. The Christian Register, 84 (9 November), 1258.
The reviewer summarizes the plot and notes that the stories originated in the fourteenth, fifteenth, and sixteenth centuries.

6 ANON. "Books and Authors." Chicago Evening Post (14 November), p. 7.
The reviewer has praise for the physical make-up of The Line of Love, which is one of the more handsome books of the season.

7 ANON. "Books and Authors." New York Sun (15 November), p. 9.
The reviewer reports the contents of The Line of Love and notes that President Theodore Roosevelt sent Cabell a personal letter of approval of it.

1905

8 ANON. Review of The Line of Love. Outlook, 81 (18 November), 682.
Although the tapestry of the book is rich, as a whole it is somewhat threadbare.

9 ANON. "On the Book Table." The Advance, 50 (30 November), 647.
In The Line of Love, "The spirit of the passionate romantic Middle Ages in France and England has been beautifully preserved.... The love scenes are fascinating."

10 ANON. Review of The Line of Love. The American Monthly Review of Reviews, 32 (December), 752.
In this volume, which is "a sumptuous holiday book of love stories," Cabell "has given us a collection, told in exquisite poetical way, of some of the most picturesque but less-known love-stories of history."

11 ANON. Review of The Line of Love. The Dial, 39 (1 December), 385.
The reviewer praises Howard Pyle's illustrations.

12 ANON. Review of The Line of Love. New York Times Holiday Book Number (1 December), p. 824.
In this book, "The story is full of incident and glows with color and life."

13 ANON. "Books of the Day." Boston Evening Transcript (2 December), 3, p. 4.
In The Line of Love, Cabell is able to evoke the spirit of the middle ages in an authoritative way. This book is one of the best of the Christmas season.

14 ANON. "Fiction in Gala Dress." Chicago Record-Herald (2 December), p. 2.
Howard Pyle's illustrations for The Line of Love receive the primary attention of the reviewer. The stories in the book have "a surprising kernel of very good reading" in them.

15 ANON. Review of The Line of Love. Chicago Inter-Ocean (9 December), p. 5.
The book will "warm the cockles of the reader's heart."

16 ANON. Review of The Line of Love. The Independent, 59 (14 December), 1378.
"The Line of Love is a love story, pure and simple."

1905

17 ANON. Review of The Line of Love. North American (15 December), p. 13.
The book evidences an author who has a "dainty and mocking touch." In its whole conception it "is absolutely unique, and the love scenes are fascinating."

18 ANON. "Books of the Day." Boston Evening Transcript (20 December), p. 18.
Howard Pyle's illustrations for The Line of Love are deftly executed, but Cabell's language is "so consistently obsolete" as to confuse the reader.

19 LEE, CARLTON. "Literature." Baltimore Sun (26 October), p. 7.
The Line of Love is a book that has much romantic charm, and the archaic language used by Cabell fits well the style of the stories.

20 McARTHUR, JAMES. "Books and Bookmen." Harper's Weekly, 49 (4 November), 1598.
After giving the plot of The Line of Love, the reviewer notes that Cabell's growing popularity is in the vein of romanticism.

21 PEATTIE, ELIZABETH W. "Imitations of Old French Tales." Chicago Daily Tribune (25 November), p. 10.
In The Line of Love, Cabell has portrayed perfectly the middle ages. "The inevitable sentiments and phrases of the [fourteenth and fifteenth centuries] are in these formal yet spontaneous tales."

1906 A BOOKS--NONE

1906 B SHORTER WRITINGS

1 ANON. Review of The Line of Love. Critic, 48 (January), 92.
The book is "an interesting contribution to romantic literature, not beyond popular understanding...."

*2 ANON. Review of The Line of Love. Western Christian Advocate, 72 (January).
Unlocatable, except as a clipping in the author's personal scrapbook.

3 TYLER, ALICE M. "Lesser Literary Centers of America: V, Richmond, Virginia." Book News, 24 (March), 482-488.

In a general survey of Richmond's current writers, the author notes that Cabell "has created, as an author, a role for himself that belongs to him individually and exclusively and that has won for him commendation" from a number of leading critics.

1907 A BOOKS--NONE

1907 B SHORTER WRITINGS

1 ANON. "New Books." New York Sun (16 October), p. 8.
Gallantry is a strange book in the way in which its author uses a blend of modern and archaic styles.

2 ANON. "New Books." New York Sun (19 October), p. 6.
Gallantry is an inconsistent book because the author does not maintain his stilted style throughout the narrative.

3 ANON. "Current Fiction." The Nation, 85 (7 November), 423-424.
Gallantry is a book whose contents are marked by cleverness, tact, and invention.

4 ANON. "Literary News and Reviews." New York Evening Post Saturday Supplement (9 November), p. 7.
Gallantry is a book which deserves praise for its "cleverness, tact, and invention."

5 ANON. Review of Gallantry. The Christian Register (14 November), p. 1300.
Plot summary, followed by the statement that the book is an edited collection of earlier stories.

6 ANON. "Writers and Books." Boston Evening Transcript (27 November), p. 24.
Gallantry is a light book that was designed for the "holiday eye" and the "holiday mind."

7 ANON. "In the Realm of Books." Chicago Record-Herald (30 November), p. 6.
Gallantry is a book that is composed of a series of stories that are "tender and brilliant."

8 ANON. Review of Gallantry. The Dial, 43 (1 December), 380-381.

1907

The stories that make up the book "are studies of temperament, of epochs, of 'precious' stylistic effects; but the story-interest invariably remains strong."

9 ANON. "Howard Pyle Illustrates 'Gallantry.'" New York Times Holiday Book Number (6 December), 1, p. 783.
Howard Pyle's illustrations are the best parts of the book, which is "slight but not uninteresting...."

10 MARCOSSON, ISAAC F. "James Branch Cabell," in Library of Southern Literature. Edited by Edwin Anderson Alderman and Joel Chandler Harris. Volume 2. New Orleans, Louisiana: Martin and Hoyt, p. 609.
The writer presents a general biographical and critical introduction to Cabell and his works, concluding that, "To read most of his stories...is to get the impression of having seen a pageant from the Arthurian days."

1909 A BOOKS--NONE

1909 B SHORTER WRITINGS

1 ANON. Review of The Cords of Vanity. New York Evening Sun (27 March), p. 6.
The book is poorly done. It opens "without plot," and continues "without rhyme or reason...."

2 ANON. Review of The Cords of Vanity. New York Times Saturday Review of Books (27 March), p. 175.
The Cords of Vanity is an unwholesome book with a sordid theme.

3 ANON. "News and Views of Books." New York World (3 April), p. 7.
The Cords of Vanity is an unpleasant book to read. It leaves "a bad taste in the mouth."

4 ANON. Review of The Cords of Vanity. Chicago Daily Tribune (7 April), p. 13.
The book "is nothing if not clever."

5 ANON. "Books of the Day." Boston Evening Transcript (7 April), p. 24.
The Cords of Vanity is aimed at a distinct reading audience. "For the sophisticated the book will be a real delight."

1909

6 ANON. "Books and Bookmen." New York Press (28 April), p. 5.
The Cords of Vanity is a difficult book to comprehend. In the main it is "vague and meaningless."

*7 ANON. Review of The Cords of Vanity. The Book News Monthly, 27 (May).
The book is urbane and sophisticated. Thematically, it "is an amusing, clever sort of study in the psychology of love." Unlocatable, except as a clipping in the author's personal scrapbook.

8 ANON. "Current Fiction." The Nation, 88 (10 June), 582.
The Cords of Vanity is not a pleasant book to read.

9 ANON. "New Books." New York Sun (12 June), p. 7.
Plot summary of The Cords of Vanity.

10 ANON. Review of The Cords of Vanity. Athenaeum (25 September), p. 357.
Cabell "exhibits wit, grace, and cleverness in devising situations" in the book. Moreover, he makes "the most of them, but the book is derivative of Oscar Wilde."

11 ANON. "A Book of the Love Business of Queens." New York American (13 November), p. 9.
"Mr. Cabell has our thanks for this seemly presentation of the old rose-scented romances," in Chivalry.

12 ANON. "Books and the Men Who Make Them." Chicago Inter-Ocean (13 November), p. 5.
The reviewer briefly retells the plot of Chivalry and concludes, "Very pleasant diverting reading these tales make." In addition, their author has a good prose style.

13 ANON. "Glimpses of the Newest Books." St. Louis Globe Democrat (20 November), p. 6.
"'Chivalry' is a book of excellent romantic qualities. It will remind the reader a little of 'The Arabian Nights' ...and 'Don Quixote.'"

14 ANON. "News and Views in the World of Books." New York World (20 November), p. 8.
Plot summary of Chivalry.

15 ANON. "Stories of the Novels." New York Post (27 November), p. 7.
Plot summary of Chivalry.

1909

16 ANON. "In the Realm of Books." Chicago Record Herald (27 November), p. 9.
Chivalry is "a most delightful volume for such as have true and youthful hearts."

17 ANON. "Recent Fiction." New York Sun (27 November), p. 10.
Writing of the characters in Chivalry, the reviewer finds that, "Had they lived in happier...times...they would have established residence in Reno," Nevada.

18 ANON. "Books of the Day." Boston Evening Transcript (1 December), p. 25.
"The ten short novels which form" Chivalry "are of exceptional charm and power."

19 ANON. Review of Chivalry. The Outlook, 93 (4 December), 787.
In Chivalry, "the stories about queens will be best appreciated by those younger readers of a larger growth who feel the fascination of a world of dames and kings and squires and jongleurs...."

20 ANON. Review of Chivalry. Brooklyn Daily Standard (5 December), 2, p. 8.
Chivalry is a most well prepared book. In particular, the romances presented here are "altogether delightful."

21 ANON. "Romances of Mediaeval France." Chicago Daily Tribune (11 December), p. 17.
The reviewer summarizes the plots of the various tales in Chivalry, noting that the book is "one of the attractive volumes of the season." Both the characters and the settings exude charm.

22 ANON. "Books and Authors." The Living Age, 45 (11 December), 701.
The reviewer of Chivalry finds that Cabell has added much to the tales in retelling them from the originals.

23 ANON. Review of Chivalry. The Dial, 47 (16 December), 520-521.
The ten stories that make up Chivalry offer "tense and tragic situations aplenty, and each brings out some heroic sacrifice."

24 ANON. "Books of the Week." New York Globe (18 December), p. 6.
Both in planning and composing Chivalry Cabell has preserved the flavor of the old days.

25 ANON. Review of Chivalry. Brooklyn Times (18 December), 2, p. 3.
The book is steeped in medieval atmosphere.

26 HAYNIE, HENRY. Review of The Cords of Vanity. Boston Times (3 April), p. 16.
Plot summary of The Cords of Vanity.

27 MARKHAM, EDWIN. "The Artistic Temperament Again." New York American (12 June), p. 9.
We learn from The Cords of Vanity that the hero Robert Townsend is an "inveterate sensation seeker, the kind of man with whom we do not wish to associate."

28 MENCKEN, H. L. Review of The Cords of Vanity. Smart Set (June), 155-156.
"There is a certain flimsiness in the plan of" The Cords of Vanity. But because of its originality and humor, "it stands head and shoulders above the common run of department store fiction. Altogether, the author shows the talent of a true craftsman."

29 REED, F. DANA. "A Sheaf of Romances." Brooklyn Daily Eagle (20 November), p. 5.
Chivalry is "evidently intended as a souvenir for holiday purposes, and it is well adapted to that end."

30 SESSIONS, ARCHIBALD LOWERY. "For Book Lovers." Ainslee's Magazine, 23 (July), 175-176.
"Mr. Cabell has chosen a very unpleasant theme for his book and a most disreputable character for his hero" in The Cords of Vanity. However, he has "shown an artistic love of good workmanship."

1910 A BOOKS--NONE

1910 B SHORTER WRITINGS

1 ANON. "Views and Reviews." Boston Herald (1 January), p. 7.
Chivalry is an excellent gift book, one that is filled with charm both in the stories and in Howard Pyle's illustrations.

2 ANON. "Royal Love Tales." Baltimore Evening Sun (6 March), p. 21.
Plot summary of Chivalry.

1913

1913 A BOOKS--NONE

1913 B SHORTER WRITINGS

1 ANON. "Books and Literary News." Chicago Inter-Ocean (20 September), p. 5.
In The Soul of Melicent, "Mr. Cabell's version of Perion and Melicent's love story [is] true, high and practically flawless art."

2 ANON. Review of The Soul of Melicent. New York Times Review of Books (28 September), p. 500.
After being questioned by the citizens of Caen, France, Cabell admitted that he had created both the stories and their supposed historic author for The Soul of Melicent.

3 ANON. "News of the Latest Books." New York American (4 October), p. 7.
The Soul of Melicent "is a book which ought to find a place in the heart of everyone who has a niche set apart therein for the glorification of love."

4 ANON. "Simple, Full of Action." Boston Globe (4 October), p. 4.
After retelling the plot of The Soul of Melicent, the reviewer notes that, "the tale is simple, but full of stirring action to the end."

5 ANON. Review of The Soul of Melicent. New York Evening Post (29 October), p. 6.
The reviewer retells the plot of The Soul of Melicent and notes that, "in both substance and form the story is far removed from the matter-of-fact atmosphere of the twentieth century."

6 ANON. Review of The Soul of Melicent. Brooklyn Daily Eagle (1 November), p. 5.
The reviewer praises the style of the book, which he finds to be particularly poetic. But he notes that, in general, the book's "appeal will be rather limited."

*7 ANON. Review of The Soul of Melicent. Brooklyn Citizen (16 November).
The reviewer retells the plot of the book, concluding that it is "a story to stir the pulses, to thrill into life the romance that sleeps in the veins of even the most sluggish." Unlocatable, except as a clipping in the author's personal scrapbook.

8 RUNYON, DAMON. "Runyan Writes of a Writer." New York <u>American</u> (15 December), p. 18.
Runyon finds that Cabell is a master craftsman of prose.

9 TOWNE, CHARLES HANSON. "The Tower Window." Cincinnati <u>Enquirer</u> (13 December), p. 10.
In <u>The Soul of Melicent</u>, Cabell exhibits an individual style, and with it he has produced "a vigorous rush and roar of splendid action that sweeps you on to a quiet but brilliant conclusion."

1914 A BOOKS--NONE

1914 B SHORTER WRITINGS

1 ANON. Review of <u>The Soul of Melicent</u>. <u>The Atlantic Monthly</u>, 113 (April), 496.
In this book Cabell's tasteful handling of the love theme is praiseworthy.

2 ANON. Review of <u>The Soul of Melicent</u>. <u>Athenaeum</u> (8 August), p. 178.
Plot summary of <u>The Soul of Melicent</u>.

1915 A BOOKS--NONE

1915 B SHORTER WRITINGS

1 ANON. <u>Little Verses and Big Names</u>. New York: George H. Doran, 305 pp.
Cabell contributed a sonnet to this volume, which identifies his work as reflecting "the splendor of the aristocratic days of the past."

2 ANON. Review of <u>The Rivet in Grandfather's Neck</u>. Springfield Massachusetts, <u>Republican</u> (14 November), p. 15.
"Many readers" of this book "will probably appreciate that the book is, as the publishers say, a novel of the passing South."

3 ANON. "Romantic Realisms." <u>The Nation</u>, 101 (18 November), 600.
In <u>The Rivet in Grandfather's Neck</u>, Cabell is attempting to "dissect your old-fashioned Southern gentleman...."

1915

4 ANON. "Mr. Cabell's Comedy." New York Times Review of Books (28 November), p. 476.
The reviewer finds that The Rivet in Grandfather's Neck is an "unusual book, and one that does not yield up its significance upon a single reading."

5 ANON. Review of The Certain Hour. The Dial, 61 (30 November), 469.
One finds from reading the book that Cabell is an "inspired artist" and a "master story-teller."

6 ANON. "James Branch Cabell's Vogue Spreads as Critics Praise Merit of His Work." Richmond News Leader (13 December), p. 10.
Upon the occasion of the publication of The Rivet in Grandfather's Neck, the writer notes that Cabell is "better known and appreciated in Boston, London and San Francisco than in his own native Richmond."

7 KERFOOT, J. B. Review of The Rivet in Grandfather's Neck. Life, 66 (18 November), 962.
The reviewer finds that the book is a "gallant yet biting tragedy of satirical realism...."

1916 A BOOKS--NONE

1916 B SHORTER WRITINGS

1 ANON. Review of The Rivet in Grandfather's Neck. Literary Digest, 52 (22 January), 185.
This is a puzzling book. "Just as the reader thinks he has caught the meaning of the story, a new idea appears, and again he searches between the lines for the real motive."

2 ANON. Review of The Certain Hour. Independent, 88 (20 November), 330.
The reviewer acknowledges the recent appearance of the book, saying that it is "prefaced by a fatuous essay."

3 C[LOVER], S[AMUEL] T. "New Books Reviewed." Richmond Evening Journal (18 November), p. 12.
The Certain Hour whets the reviewer's appetite to read more of Cabell.

1917 A BOOKS--NONE

1917 B SHORTER WRITINGS

1 ANON. "Notable Volumes of Short Stories." New York Times Review of Books (14 January), p. 13.
The Certain Hour is a particularly welcome book because of its romantic quality in a day when fiction is too realistic.

2 ANON. Review of The Cream of the Jest. New York Times Review of Books (7 October), p. 380.
Regarding this book, the reviewer surmises that Cabell must have "loved" writing it. The reviewer notes also that the book is aimed at a minority of the reading audience.

3 ANON. "Books of the Day." Boston Evening Transcript (15 November), p. 13.
In reviewing The Cream of the Jest, the writer is impressed by Cabell's "masterly interpretation of the tragedy of a man living in dreams, who is nevertheless condemned to do so many distasteful things" in daily life.

4 ANON. "Books of Interest." New York Sun (15 December), p. 6.
The reviewer fears that there are many readers who will recognize that The Cream of the Jest "contains true gold," but who "will grudge the mental labor involved in getting it out."

5 ANON. "Books." Boston Herald (29 December), p. 10.
The reviewer concludes that The Cream of the Jest is "no story for the plodder, but delightful reading for one of lively imagination."

6 C[LOVER], S[AMUEL] T. "New Books Reviewed." Richmond Evening Journal (6 October), p. 6.
The reviewer provides a plot summary of The Cream of the Jest and then goes on to praise Cabell's wit, especially what he says regarding publishers.

7 C[LOVER], S[AMUEL] T. "New Books Reviewed." Richmond Evening Journal (13 October), p. 4.
The reviewer deciphers the sigil that Cabell devised as a key to The Cream of the Jest.

8 GALANTIÈRE, LEWIS. "Hm!--Let's See." Chicago Examiner (15 December), p. 6.

1917

After finding The Cream of the Jest to be "an exquisite fantasy," the reviewer goes on to say that Cabell "is writing the loveliest prose of any living writer in English known to me."

9 MORLEY, CHRISTOPHER. "The Teacher's Bookshelf." Educational Foundations (February), pp. 366-369.
In The Certain Hour, Cabell reveals himself as "really an Elizabethan who finds himself something at odds with our hubble-bubble democracy.... Those who delight in the finer sensations of literature will find an ordinate satisfaction in his very delicate stories."

10 RASCOE, BURTON. "Here's a Chance to Own Another First Edition." Chicago Daily Tribune (29 December), p. 9.
The Cream of the Jest is "without question, the one book of the period in English most certain to enjoy permanent favor with those to whom delicate whimsy, irony, an intelligent point of view, nuance, and subtleties of expression are the highest desiderata in an author."

11 ROGERS, J. M. Review of From the Hidden Way. Book News Monthly (17 January), pp. 203-204.
In this book, "Mr. Cabell is in the twilight zone of moderate poets. He has not wholly gone over to the Vorticists and the Modernists and the Realists, but he has invaded that realm...."

1918 A BOOKS

1 MENCKEN, H. L. Mr. Cabell of Virginia. New York: Robert M. McBride, 8 pp.
This leaflet contains a general critical appraisal of Cabell and his works, concluding that what he writes "is very rare in America." Appeared also in the New York Evening Mail (3 July).

1918 B SHORTER WRITINGS

1 ANON. "Author and Publisher." New York Tribune (12 January), p. 7.
The reviewer finds The Cream of the Jest to be "a curious rambling story, without form, and told in a sort of blundering, disorderly fashion."

1918

2 ANON. Review of The Cream of the Jest. Springfield, Massachusetts, Sunday Republican (13 January), p. 15.
"Both for its originality and value the book is notable."

3 B., S. Review of The Cream of the Jest. The New Republic, 16 (26 October), 377-378.
In this book, Cabell deserves praise for his wit and use of irony; however, he is not unequivocally admired.

4 FOLLET, WILSON. "A Gossip on James Branch Cabell." The Dial, 64 (25 April), 392-396.
A general article on Cabell, concluding that "he is a romancer only by the most superficial of all the distinctions that can be drawn. Basically he is a realist without the astigmatism of the localist and the modernist, and without their expert and industrious provision for a quick oblivion."

5 HECHT, BEN. "Concerning James Branch Cabell." Chicago Daily News (10 April), p. 12.
In a combined review of The Rivet in Grandfather's Neck, The Cream of the Jest, The Hidden Way, and The Certain Hour, the reviewer finds that Cabell is "...worthy of a niche in the high roosting places of the gargoyles."

6 HUGHES, RUPERT. "Literature and Life." Chicago Tribune (27 April), p. 9.
The author, after noting the Tribune's "spring drive... in behalf of James Branch Cabell," takes Cabell to task for the false impression of Greek life in an earlier Tribune article.

7 HUGHES, RUPERT. "Anti-Cabellum." Chicago Tribune (18 May), p. 11.
The author defends himself against Cabell's earlier attacks on him.

8 RASCOE, BURTON. "On a Certain Condescension in Our Natives." Chicago Tribune (16 February), p. 9.
In a general article about current American writing, the author notes the neglect accorded to Cabell.

9 RASCOE, BURTON. "Convent." Chicago Tribune (2 March), p. 9.
Reviewer Stanley Braithwaite was taken in by Cabell's fictitious trubador poets invented for From the Hidden Way.

10 RASCOE, BURTON. "Presuming You Are Interested." Chicago Tribune (16 March), p. 9.

1918

While reviewing Helen Thomas Follet and Wilson Follett's Modern Novelists, the writer comments on Cabell's not being included even though he is "as great as anyone now writing in English."

11 RASCOE, BURTON. "An Approach to James Branch Cabell." Chicago Tribune (6 April), p. 12.
In an extended appraisal of Cabell's works, the writer compares him favorably to Charles Lamb, Walter Pater, William Congreve, Theophile Gautier, Anatole France, and Jean Baptiste Molière.

12 RASCOE, BURTON. "Presuming You Are Interested." Chicago Tribune (20 April), p. 11.
In an extended article on Cabell, the author defends his fulsome praise and support of him.

*13 MENCKEN, H. L. "A Sub-Potomac Phenomenon." Smart Set (August).
Unlocatable, cited in Brewer, 1957.A1.

1919 A BOOKS--NONE

1919 B SHORTER WRITINGS

1 A., M. "Escaping From Life." The New Republic, 18 (26 April), 430-431.
Cabell's world view is unsound, as a critic of both literature and of life. This is apparent from reading Beyond Life.

2 ANON. "News and Reviews of Interesting Books." New York Herald (19 January), 3, p. 7.
In Beyond Life, one cannot help wondering if Cabell is not sometimes insincere. Nevertheless, "we may welcome him into the...ranks of American essayists."

3 ANON. "The Able Critic." Boston Herald (25 January), p. 5.
Beyond Life "is a rich book for thoughtful readers."

4 ANON. "Notable Books." New York Times Review of Books (26 January), p. 39.
Cabell "seeks an ivory tower" in which to hide from the world, but he "is never bitter"; rather, he has "a sly and delightful humor."

1919

5 ANON. "Let's Give Romance a Chance." New York Tribune Review (9 February), p. 6.
The editor reprints a generous section of Beyond Life.

6 ANON. "Does Man Live by Lying?" New York World (9 February), E, p. 6.
Beyond Life is a book that suggests that man lives by deception. As Cabell himself states it, "man's sole business...is to lie to himself...as artistically as possible."

7 ANON. Review of Beyond Life. The Nation, 108 (22 February), 289.
Beyond Life affords the reader a good view of Cabell's "unflinching iconoclasm."

8 ANON. "Reviews of New Books." Literary Digest, 60 (22 March), 49.
Cabell sometimes shows "sophomoric erudition" in Beyond Life; nevertheless, the book offers "a good ten hours of intellectual stimulation."

9 ANON. "James Branch Cabell: Cynical Champion of a Romantic Cosmos." Current Opinion, 66 (April), 254-255.
The reviewer is pleased to find that in Beyond Life one finds an emerging romanticist in an age given over to literary realism.

10 ANON. "Popular Author's View of Literature." Richmond Evening Journal (11 April), p. 1.
In an interview, Joseph Hergesheimer praises Cabell as one of the greatest writers of the contemporary South.

11 ANON. "The New Books." Review of Reviews, 59 (May), 555.
In Beyond Life, both the style and the use of symbolism are praiseworthy.

*12 ANON. Review of Beyond Life. The Churchman (7 June).
"We have read in [Beyond Life] and conclude that those who like garrulity will like it. We regret to say, we don't." Unlocatable, except as a clipping in the author's personal scrapbook.

13 ANON. "The Scream [sic] of the Jest." New York Sun Books and the Book World (20 July), p. 5.
The author provides a general article on Cabell's rising reputation, finding him "one of the few first-rate literary craftsmen of our day."

1919

14 ANON. Review of Jurgen. New York Times Review of Books (28 September), p. 494.
In this novel, Cabell has "become the willing slave of quaint fancy, fecund inventiveness, and unleashed imagination."

15 ANON. "Books in Particular." New York Globe (3 October), p. 17.
Jurgen is similar to James Stephens' The Crock of Gold.

*16 "B., L. V." [MARGARET LEE]. "Ainslee's Book of the Month." Ainslee's Magazine (November).
Jurgen is a book that has "sweep and breadth.... Its background is the universe with all its best possible worlds." Unlocatable, except as a clipping in the author's personal scrapbook.

17 BOYNTON, H. W. "Masculine Comedy." The Review, 1 (25 October), 1.
Jurgen is a book that has a great deal of beauty; however, Cabell uses too much "erotic symbolism."

18 BROUN, HEYWOOD. Review of Jurgen. New York Tribune (17 November), p. 8.
"Mr. Cabell has not a sufficiently free and rich imagination to animate his fantastic tale throughout." The story is a "barroom story refurbished for the boudoir."

19 BROUN, HEYWOOD. "Peeks Among Peakes." New York Tribune (29 November), p. 9.
In a general article on current writers, the author finds that Cabell is too immoral in Jurgen.

20 C[LOVER], S[AMUEL] T. "New Books Reviewed." Richmond Evening Journal (11 January), p. 7.
Cabell should pay attention to the critics who are opposed to him. Nevertheless, he has a keen wit and a classical style.

21 C[LOVER], S[AMUEL] T. "New Books Reviewed." Richmond Evening Journal (11 October), p. 7.
In Jurgen, Cabell compares favorably with George Bernard Shaw.

22 C., W. H. "'Jurgen' a Brilliant Book." New York Tribune (18 October), p. 10.
In Jurgen, Cabell deftly handles such elements as satire, charm, description, and fantasy. In addition, he makes dramatic use of sex.

23 D., N. P. "The New Books." New York Globe and Commercial Advertiser (11 January), p. 8.
Beyond Life is a book that has a number of themes, many of which the reviewer explains.

24 D., N. P. "The New Books." New York Globe (22 February), p. 8.
The reviewer quotes from Beyond Life in order to illustrate Cabell's concept of posterity.

25 D., N. P. "The New Books." New York Globe (20 December), p. 10.
The reviewer finds Jurgen to be similar to James Stephens' The Crock of Gold.

26 FOLLETT, WILSON. "Ten Times One Makes One." The Dial, 66 (8 March), 225-228.
In reviewing Beyond Life, the author takes the occasion to write a general article on Cabell and his works. He concludes that "Mr. Cabell is one of the very few living writers who have offered hostages to nothing in space or time except...ultravitality."

27 GORDON, GEORGE. "James Branch Cabell," in The Men Who Make Our Novels. New York: Moffat, Yard, pp. 113-118.
The author summarizes several of Cabell's novels and then presents a brief biographical sketch of him.

28 HERGESHEIMER, JOSEPH. "An Improvisation on Themes From 'Jurgen.'" New York Sun (26 October), p. 4.
In reviewing the novel, the author finds that "All the fabulous loveliness that has drugged men with rapture and death returns in the magic of 'Jurgen.'"

29 LAPPIN, HENRY A. "Romance of the Demiurge." The Bookman, 49 (April), 220-222.
In reviewing Beyond Life, the author finds that "If Mr. Cabell were an Englishman, an Irishman, or a translated Frenchman he would have long before this have been monographed and lectured upon by...professors.... For, with rare lapses, Mr. Cabell is no less scholar than artist."

30 NEWBERGER, LOUIS. "Cabell." Chicago Daily News (9 April), p. 12.
In reviewing The Rivet in Grandfather's Neck, the writer finds it to be not so good as Cabell's earlier novels. It "performs the same services as...'Spoon River Anthology.'"

1919

31 PRESTON, KEITH. "The Periscope." Chicago Daily News (29 October), p. 12.
In general, Cabell is too complex, but in Jurgen there can be found suavity, brilliance, and beauty. Moreover, the book has "the spirit of mischief."

32 RASCOE, BURTON. "Jim and Joe Author a One-Act Play Which Lacks Punch or Point." Chicago Tribune (1 February), p. 13.
The writer presents imaginary dialogue between Cabell and Joseph Hergesheimer as two of the most popular authors of the day.

33 RASCOE, BURTON. "A Note on 'Jurgen' by James Branch Cabell." Chicago Tribune (11 October), p. 12.
The author comments on numerous aspects of the novel after having read it nine times, "parts of it" more than that.

34 SCARBOROUGH, DOROTHY. "Life and James Branch Cabell." New York Sun Books and Book World (2 February), p. 1.
Plot summary of Beyond Life, followed by comments upon Cabell's current and rising reputation.

35 W., L. C. "A 'Poseur' Speaks." New York Tribune (29 March), p. 10.
Beyond Life "is not one of the noteworthy and thoughtful books of these years."

36 WALPOLE, HUGH. "Why Not Cheer the Millennium Along?" New York Sun Books and the Book World (16 November), p. 9.
In a general appraisal of contemporary writing, the author makes passing references to Cabell as being a major writer.

1920 A BOOKS

1 ANON. Jurgen and the Censor. New York: Privately Printed for E. H. Bierstadt, 77 pp.
This study is comprised of the report to the Emergency Committee, formed to protest the suppression of Jurgen.

2 WALPOLE, HUGH. The Art of James Branch Cabell. New York: Robert M. McBride, 32 pp.
In this pamphlet, the author provides an overview of Cabell's works to date. Revised and reprinted 1925.A3; reprinted 1967.B23.

1920 B SHORTER WRITINGS

*1 A., J. Review of Jurgen. Pearson's Magazine (June).
In Jurgen, Cabell's "idea is evidently to entertain rather than to advance a serious view of existence." Unlocatable, except as a clipping in the author's personal scrapbook.

2 ANON. "Author of 'Jurgen' Outguesses Vice Society." New York Tribune Magazine and Book Section (28 November), p. 9.
Cabell's Domnei is a book in which the author's artistry "is of a degree that demands superlative terms in comment."

*3 ANON. "Cabell's Novel Which Needs no Censor." Brooklyn Daily Eagle (11 December).
The reviewer has doubts that Cabell's Domnei is an authentically medieval work. Unlocatable, except as a clipping in the author's personal scrapbook.

4 ANON. "Woman Supreme: A Mediaeval View." New York Sun (31 December), p. 11.
In Domnei, Cabell's greatest achievement lies in the way in which he preserves the medieval concept of knightly love.

5 BENCHLEY, ROBERT C. "Books and Other Things." New York World (14 February), p. 8.
Jurgen is no more than "a frank imitation of the old-time pornographers."

6 BENCHLEY, ROBERT C. "Books and Other Things." New York World (15 December), p. 14.
In his attempts to defend Jurgen in "The Taboo in Literature" Cabell presents a specious argument.

7 BROUN, HEYWOOD. "More Meddling by the Censor." New York Tribune (17 January), p. 11.
In this news story, the author outlines the legal charges brought against Jurgen.

8 BROUN, HEYWOOD. "Books." New York Tribune (28 January), p. 12.
The author reproduces large sections of a letter from John S. Sumner regarding Jurgen.

9 CANNAN, GILBERT. "'The Rainbow' and 'Jurgen.'" New York Tribune Magazine and Book Section (8 February), p. 11.
The author provides a general discussion of censorship and then particularly relates it to D. H. Lawrence's The Rainbow and to Jurgen.

1920

10 CLOVER, SAMUEL T. "Jurgen and the Tumblebug." Richmond Evening Journal (10 February), p. 6.
The author writes a parody of Jurgen, for which he asks justice.

11 DeCASSERES, BENJAMIN. "As to Collaboration." New York Evening Post Spring Book Review (24 April), p. 15.
In a general article about contemporary writing, the author points to Jurgen as being different from the mainstream.

12 DeCASSERES, BENJAMIN. "The Romantic Irony of Cabell." New York Evening Post Literary Review (26 June), p. 3.
Cabell "stands apart in the literature of America today.... He may be the beginning of a great reaction in our mode of looking at things."

13 DeCASSERES, BENJAMIN. "What the Postman Blew Out of His Whistle." Judge (11 December), p. 10.
The author comments on the suppression of Jurgen.

14 GUNTHER, JOHN J. "James Branch Cabell: An Introduction." The Bookman, 52 (November), 200-206.
The author provides a general appraisal of Cabell's works, concluding that "It would be a rash critic who would declare him the most important figure in contemporary American letters, but an exceedingly conservative one who would not grant him to be the most interesting."

15 HAMMOND, PERCY. "Jurgen and the Censor." Chicago Tribune (2 October), p. 9.
The author provides a general discussion of the moral and social problems brought on by the act of censorship. He then relates the problem in general to the suppression of Jurgen.

16 KINGSLEY, WALTER J. "About a Column." New York Tribune (3 January), p. 7.
Jurgen, the reviewer concludes, is heavily laden with sex.

17 KINGSLEY, WALTER J. "About a Column." New York Tribune Magazine and Book Section (15 February), p. 11.
The author reprints a letter from Sinclair Lewis in which he expresses shock that Jurgen has been suppressed.

18 LAPPIN, HENRY A. "A Shelf of New Books." The Bookman, 50 (January), 485-486.

Although the future may discover Cabell's greatness, the current general reading public seems unmoved by Jurgen.

19 LeGALLIENNE, RICHARD. "James Branch Cabell, Master of the Pastiche." New York Times (13 February), p. 3.
Cabell is a writer who masquerades in the ideas of others.

20 M., D. L. Review of The Cream of the Jest. Boston Evening Transcript (25 August), 2, p. 6.
In this book, Cabell reveals himself as a great artist; moreover, he is one who has a great knowledge of literature, philosophy, and history.

21 MENCKEN, H. L. "On American Letters." Baltimore Evening Sun (25 October), p. 8.
Although Cabell's books have a kind of delicacy about them, Cabell displayed a marked toughness when confronted by the censors in the matter of Jurgen.

22 MUNSON, GORHAM B. "The Professional Smuthounds." New York Tribune (26 March), p. 12.
In a letter to the editor, the author protests the suppression of Jurgen.

*23 STAGNELL, GREGORY. "Discovered by the Censor." The New York Medical Journal (24 July).
In a review of The Cream of the Jest and Beyond Life, the author finds that Cabell is "one of the really great writers of the present day." Unlocatable, except as a clipping in the author's personal scrapbook.

24 WILLIAMS, BLANCHE COLTON. "James Branch Cabell," in her Our Short Story Writers. New York: Moffat, Yard, pp. 22-40.
The author provides a discussion of Cabell the artist as he is perceived from his books.

1921 A BOOKS

1 JOHNSON, MERLE. A Bibliographic Check List of the Works of James Branch Cabell, 1904-1921. New York: Frank Shay, 27 pp.
The compiler describes and provides textual notes on all Cabell books through 1921.

1921

1921 B SHORTER WRITINGS

1 ANON. "Mr. Cabell of Virginia." The Double Dealer, 1 (January), 5-7.
The author defends Cabell, after his being attacked by John J. Gunther in the pages of The Bookman, 1920.B14.

2 ANON. "Views and News of the World of Books." New York World (2 January), E, p. 11.
Domnei is indeed "a marvellously absorbing tale."

3 ANON. "Cabell Rewrites Another Novel." New York Tribune Magazine and Book Section (16 January), p. 8.
In writing about the reissue of The Cream of the Jest, the reviewer notes that the original publication was not well received.

4 ANON. "James Branch Cabell: Master of Shady Romance." Kansas City Star (19 February), p. 10.
The author comments generally upon Cabell's contribution to literature, making specific references to Jurgen.

5 ANON. "James Branch Cabell Plays Hide and Seek With the Censors." New York Tribune Magazine and Book Section (27 February), p. 8.
Cabell is not as frank about sexual matters in Figures of Earth as he was in Jurgen.

6 ANON. Review of The Cords of Vanity. The Outlook, 127 (2 March), 347.
The Cords of Vanity is a "new edition of one of Mr. Cabell's less important novels, which has been improved by a thorough rewriting, but is not yet as well centered and vital as is the original."

7 ANON. "Latest Works of Fiction." New York Times Book Review and Magazine (6 March), p. 22.
Figures of Earth is a book that is "curious, often very beautiful and at the bottom very sad."

8 ANON. "Views and News of the World of Books." New York World (6 March), E, p. 10.
In Figures of Earth, "James Branch Cabell reveals himself by turns a clown, poet, satirist and Romanticist."

9 ANON. "Is the Author of Jurgen Overestimated?" Current Opinion, 70 (April), 537-538.

The author surveys the current ideas and opinions about Cabell's works, but does not arrive at a conclusion of his own.

10 ANON. Review of Figures of Earth. Springfield, Massachusetts, Republican (13 May), p. 8.
The reviewer is pleased to find this book among the spate of the more fashionable realistic novels, but he notes that Cabell is somewhat too allegorical.

11 ANON. Review of Figures of Earth. Booklist, 17 (May-June), 302.
This is a book that "will be understood and enjoyed only by a few."

12 ANON. Review of Figures of Earth. The Dial, 71 (August), 242.
This book is "quite as naughty as Jurgen but circumnavigates more skillfully the rocks of censorship." Also, "the book is very uneven. Usually it is either overwritten or underwritten."

13 ANON. Review of The Cords of Vanity. The Dial, 71 (September), 372.
This is "the second edition of a...frequently dull novel...."

14 ANON. "Bookish Chat and Comment." Boston Herald (24 September), p. 5.
Figures of Earth is "a strange sort of book, a work of soaring fancy...."

*15 ANON. "A Reaction Against Realism." The Ladies' Field (17 December).
Unlocatable, except as a clipping in the author's scrapbook.

16 BARLOW, SAMUEL L. M. "The Censor of Art." North American Review, 213 (March), 346-350.
The author writes a general article against censorship, occasioned by the suppression of Jurgen.

17 BOYD, ERNEST. "Adult or Infantile Censorship." The Dial, 70 (April), 381-385.
In a general discussion of censorship, the author makes a number of references to the Jurgen case.

18 BOYNTON, H. W. Review of The Cream of the Jest and Domnei. Weekly Review, 4 (26 January), 85-86.

Although Cabell's fame has risen markedly since the publication of Jurgen, the reviewer wonders if books such as these, both recently re-released, should be published again.

19 BROUN, HEYWOOD. "Censoring the Censor." The Bookman, 53 (May), 193-196.
The author attacks John S. Sumner for his attempt at legally censoring Jurgen.

20 BUTCHER, FANNY. "Tabloid Book Review." Chicago Tribune (13 March), p. 7.
Figures of Earth is an epic.

21 COLUM, PADRAIC. "A Latter-Day Mediaevalist." The Freeman, 2 (5 January), 404-405.
Domnei is "a subtle story, but not a convincing story." It "never loses the quality of being an allegory."

22 COOPER, FREDERIC TABER. "Cabell Self-Expurgated." Publishers Weekly, 99 (19 February), 572.
Cabell is still suffering from the censorship of Jurgen. But the net result is that while the written text [of Figures of Earth] is spotless as a shining morning face, an alert mind can read between the lines many pungent little ironies." It would not be surprising if both books "should find their niche in posterity's Hall of Fame."

23 DAWSON, N. P. "The New Books." New York Globe (30 April), p. 6.
The reviewer discusses the suppression of Jurgen and Cabell's literary fortunes in general, not Figures of Earth--the book in question.

24 DeCASSERES, BENJAMIN. "James Branch Cabell: Prospero." Shadowland (February), pp. 41, 68.
The author compares Cabell to the great European writers.

25 DeCASSERES, BENJAMIN. "Two Cabell Novels." New York Herald Magazine and Books (25 December), p. 11.
Chivalry and The Line of Love are "the immortal stuffs of beauty, wisdom and mirth...."

26 FULLER, HENRY B. "One on a Tower." The Freeman, 3 (4 May), 186-187.
The author provides a slight appraisal of Cabell's works, concluding that he "remains a cate ambrosial for the experienced and determined adult." Reprinted 1924.B15.

27 GABRIEL, CHARLES, JR. Review of Figures of Earth. Chicago Tribune (18 September), 8, p. 13.
The reviewer compares the book to Jurgen, finding both similarities and differences.

28 GLENN, ELLIS. "Cabell: Short Story Writer." The William and Mary Literary Magazine (June), pp. 335-344.
The author provides a general appraisal of Cabell's works.

29 HECHT, BEN. "Mr. Cabell Dons the Toga." Chicago Daily News (30 March), p. 12.
Figures of Earth is "an interesting classic."

30 HEWLETT, MAURICE. "The Essentials of Nonsense." New York Evening Post Literary Review (23 April), p. 3.
Figures of Earth is nonsense and "excessively tiresome."

31 LeGALLIENE, RICHARD. "James Branch Cabell: Master of the Pastiche." New York Times Book Review and Magazine (13 February), pp. 3, 22.
The author provides a general appreciation of the entire Cabell canon.

32 LIND, JOHN E. Review of Jurgen. The Psychoanalytic Review, 8 (July), 337-338.
Jurgen "is such a story as a pagan poet might have told."

33 LOVETT, ROBERT MORSS. "Mr. James Branch Cabell." New Republic, 26 (13 April), 187-189.
The author provides a general appraisal of Cabell's works, concluding that we "are all beginning to be better" for what he has written.

34 M., D. L. Review of Figures of Earth. Boston Evening Transcript (6 April), 3, p. 4.
In this book "the often repeated phrase that 'Mr. Cabell writes only for the few' seems more than justified. He must be a dark forest for all others...."

35 McCARDELL, ROY L. "James Branch Cabell--Author of 'Jurgen.'" Morning Telegraph (New York) (21 August), 2, p. 4.
The author provides an overview of Cabell and his works.

36 MacCOLLOUGH, MARTIN. "James Branch Cabell," in his Letters on Contemporary American Authors. Boston: Four Seas, pp. 7-12.

1921

The author provides a general appreciation of Cabell's works, finding their author "the most phenomenal literary genius of his time."

37 MANN, DOROTHEA LAWRANCE. "Books of the Day." Boston Evening Transcript (8 January), 4, p. 6.
In Domnei, Cabell exhibits a profound world view and imagination.

38 MATLACK, H. W. Review of Figures of Earth and The Cords of Vanity. The Grinnell Review, 16 (June), 449-450.
Figures of Earth and The Cords of Vanity are "utterly dissimilar in style, content, and subject matter...," but each one is "quite the best thing of its particular type that contemporary fiction...affords...." But "the squeamish and the unimaginative had better leave this author's books alone...."

39 MENCKEN, H. L. "New Cabell Book Joke on Snouters." Baltimore Evening Sun (12 March), p. 6.
Figures of Earth is "chemically pure," and Cabell's long apprenticeship is over--"he is understood and esteemed."

*40 NEWMAN, FRANCES. "James Branch Cabell." Carnegie Library Quarterly (May).
Unlocatable, cited in Brewer, 1957.A1.

41 PARRINGTON, VERNON LEWIS. "The Incomparable Mr. Cabell," in his The Beginnings of Critical Realism in America. New York: Harcourt, Brace, pp. 335-345.
The author provides an in-depth appraisal of Cabell's works, concluding that he "is creating great literature.... He stands apart from the throng of lesser American novelists...." Reprinted in The Pacific Review, 2 (December), 353-366; and 1930.B10, B11; 1958.B6.

42 REDMAN, BEN RAY. "Bulg the Forgotten." The Reviewer, 2 (November), 90-94.
The author suggests a possible source for this fictional character used by Cabell.

43 STARRETT, VINCENT. "The Passing of James Branch Cabell." The Double Dealer, 2 (November), 203-209.
The author provides an extended general appraisal of Cabell's works, resting on the assumption that "No other writer of modern times has been in turn so neglected, so bepraised, and so bespattered."

1921

44 STEWART, DONALD OGDEN. "Cristofer Colombo: A Comedy of Discovery," in his A Parody Outline of History. Garden City, New York: Garden City Publishing Company, p. 230.
The author makes literary use of Cabell's style in writing a parody on Columbus.

45 SUMNER, JOHN S. "Criticising the Critic." The Bookman, 53 (July), 385-388.
In an attack upon Heywood Broun, the prosecutor of Jurgen defines his concepts of censorship.

46 THOMAS, J. A. "A Note on James Branch Cabell." Yale Literary Magazine, 86 (March), 245-247.
It is difficult to categorize Cabell's works because he "is a writer for the elect--but for the elect of all time."

47 UNTERMEYER, LOUIS. "James Branch Cabell," in his Modern American Poetry. New York: Harcourt, Brace, pp. 213-216.
The author provides a short biographical sketch of Cabell and reprints two of his poems.

48 UNTERMEYER, LOUIS. "Hark, from the Tomb!" The Reviewer, 1 (16 May), 212-213.
The author defends Cabell against an attack in print made by Maurice Hewlett.

49 VAN DOREN, CARL. "Ecclesiastes in Virginia." The Nation, 112 (9 March), 381.
Figures of Earth is "cheerful, shrewd, wise, beautiful, and learned."

50 VAN DOREN, CARL. "Contemporary American Novelists: VI: James Branch Cabell." The Nation, 112 (29 June), 914-915.
The author provides a general overview of Cabell's works.

51 VAN DOREN, CARL. "The Cabells and Their Kin." The Nation (7 December), p. 664.
The author provides a study of the revisions Cabell made for the reissue of his books in the Storisende edition.

52 W., R. D. Review of The Cream of the Jest. Boston Evening Transcript (12 February), p. 6.
Although this book has some well done parts in it, Cabell's dialogue often "shows a straining for effect, or is unnatural."

53 WEBER, HENRIETTE. "Literary Outlook." Chicago Journal of Commerce and Daily Financial Times (23 April), p. 10.

1922

In Figures of Earth Cabell deserves praise for his "high-minded application...of an old tale."

1922 A BOOKS

1 GLENN, GARRARD and WILLIAM U. GOODBODY. "Brief for Defendants on Motion to Direct an Acquittal." New York: Printed by the New York Evening Post Job Printing Office, 40 pp.
This pamphlet comprises the legal brief prepared in the defense of Guy Holt, Robert M. McBride and Company, and Robert M. McBride regarding the obscenity trial of Jurgen.

1922 B SHORTER WRITINGS

1 ANON. "Risqué and Sex Books in Biggest Vogue Here." Richmond News Leader (Clipping dated only 1922).
In this short news story, the writer notes that copies of Jurgen sometimes bring as much as twenty dollars on the black market.

2 ANON. "James Branch Cabell." The Canadian Bookman (January), p. 57.
Cabell is "one of the towering figures of American literature, typical of the best culture of the country to which he belongs...."

3 ANON. "British Reviewers on Mr. James Branch Cabell." The Living Age, 312 (March), 735-736.
The author lists briefly, using quotations, English critics' attitudes toward Jurgen.

4 ANON. "Latest Works of Fiction." New York Times Book Review and Magazine (16 July), p. 17.
Gallantry "is a delectable piece of work for all its drawbacks of dullness of style and violence of incident."

5 ASSOCIATED PRESS. "New York Jurist Finds No Objection to Cabell's Book." Richmond Times-Dispatch (20 October), p. 1.
This news story, announcing the acquittal of Jurgen, appeared in a number of newspapers.

6 BISHOP, JOHN PEALE. "The Modernism of Mr. Cabell." Vanity Fair (March), p. 16.
Cabell has much in common with modern writers, but his inadequate style is inflexible, and his visual imagination thin.

1922

7 BJÖRKMAN, EDWIN. "Concerning James Branch Cabell's Human Comedy." The Literary Digest International Book Review, 1 (December), 40 ff.

The author provides an extensive appraisal of Cabell's works, based on the premise that he is "the only one of our living literary artists in this country who has worked out something like a truly philosophic conception of human existence."

8 BLEI, FRANZ. "Cabell," in his Das Grosse Bestarium der Moderne Literatur. Berlin: Ernst Rowahlt, 252 pp.

The author briefly mentions Cabell, calling him the centaur of American literature.

9 BROUN, HEYWOOD and others. Nonsensorship. New York: G. P. Putnam's Sons, passim.

The authors include minor passing references to Cabell.

10 CHUBB, THOMAS CALDECOTT. "Books of Yesteryear: Cabell in 1904." New York Tribune (7 May), 4, p. 7.

The Eagle's Shadow, recently republished, does not portend of the later Cabell.

11 PARSHLEY, HOWARD MADISON. "Report on a Collection of Hemiptera-Heteroptera from South Dakota." Smith College Contributions from the Department of Zoology, Number 85. South Dakota State College Technical Bulletin Number 2 (April), 22 pp.

The author names a water-bug after Rhagovelia Oriander, a character in Cabell's Figures of Earth.

12 PROSPERO. "Prospero's Musings." Baltimore Evening Sun (20 March), p. 8.

The reviewer rehashes the obscenity charges levelled against Jurgen and then finds Cabell to be much like Jonathan Swift.

13 RASCOE, BURTON. "Papé's Illustrations for Cabell's 'Jurgen.'" The International Studio, 74 (January), 203-208.

The author discusses the illustrations for the English edition of Jurgen.

14 RASCOE, BURTON. "A Bookman's Daybook." New York Tribune Weekly Review of the Arts (18 June), p. 4.

The writer reproduces comments made by Cabell to H. L. Mencken on the nature of immortality.

15 RASCOE, BURTON. "A Note on James Branch Cabell." New York Tribune (6 August), p. 3.

The author provides a general appraisal of Cabell's works.

16 ROBERTSON, WILLIAM JOSEPH. "Bright Future for Literature, Writers Say." Richmond News Leader (13 May), p. 3.
The author conducts an interview with Cabell, among others, on the future promise of American literature.

17 UNTERMEYER, LOUIS. "The Heaven Above Storisende," in his Heavens. New York: Harcourt, Brace, pp. 49-60.
The author provides a brief imaginative sketch that makes literary use of Cabell's prose style.

18 UNTERMEYER, LOUIS. "A Key to Cabell." The Double Dealer, 4 (July), 29-31.
The author explains the essence of Cabell's dramatic and moral vision.

19 VAN DOREN, CARL. "James Branch Cabell," in his Contemporary American Novelists, 1900-1920. New York: Macmillan, pp. 104-113.
The author provides a general appraisal of Cabell and his position in modern fiction.

20 VAN DOREN, CARL. "Jurgen in Limbo." The Nation, 115 (6 December), 613-614.
The author writes a prose dramatization centering on the Jurgen suppression. Reprinted in The Nation, 5 (6 December), 613-614.

21 VAN VECHTEN, CARL. Peter Whiffles: His Life and Works. New York: Alfred A. Knopf, pp. 231-232.
The author provides a brief discussion of Cabell and his works, noting that he has changed from Romanticism to irony in his fiction.

22 WRIGHT, CUTHBERT. "Two Romantics." The Freeman, 5 (6 September), 621.
In Gallantry, "Mr. Cabell seems to be another writer at present engaged in somewhat monotonously exploiting a single talent."

1923 A BOOKS

1 HOLT, GUY. Jurgen and the Law: A Statement with Exhibits, Including the Court's Opinion, and the Brief for the Defendants on Motion to Direct an Acquittal. New York: Robert M. McBride.

The contents of this 78-page pamphlet are explained in the title.

1923 B SHORTER WRITINGS

1 ANON. "The Literary Spotlight: James Branch Cabell." The Bookman, 56 (February), 741-745.
The author provides biographical details about Cabell, along with an explanation of his works and his dramatic vision.

2 ANON. "Les dernières publications américaines." L'Europe Nouvelle (30 June), p. 828.
Speaking of Jurgen, the reviewer praises Cabell's imagination and his ironic style of writing.

3 ANON. "Mr. Cabell." The Triad, 8 (10 August), 41-42.
The reviewer provides a plot summary of The Cream of the Jest, after finding Cabell "the most delightful American writer now alive."

*4 ANON. Review of The Cream of the Jest. Allahabad (India) Pioneer (23 September).
Unlocatable, cited in Brewer, 1957.A1.

5 ANON. "Good Books." Time, 2 (29 October), 15.
The reissue of The Eagle's Shadow contains a story that is a "light, urbane comedy...."

6 ANON. "Flat Tasting, Luscious Looking." New York Sun and the Globe (1 December), p. 7.
In The High Place, "far the best things...are its humorously destructive presentation of certain old shams...."

*7 ANON. Review of The High Place. Brooklyn Daily Eagle (22 December).
The book is "shallow, not especially beautiful in style, tedious in allegory...and, in a word, tiresome." Unlocatable, except as clipping in author's personal scrapbook.

8 ANON. "Recent Publications Reviewed." New York Herald Tribune, Paris Edition (31 December), p. 5.
The High Place "puts Mr. Cabell at the head of the class of 'shocking writers.'"

9 ARONSON, HOWARD STANLEY. Review of The High Place. Galveston Daily News (16 December), p. 20.

In this book, "as in his others, Cabell writes of the Universal Man--he who dreams and adventures; he who is a determinist, not an altruist...."

10 BABB, STANLEY E. "James Branch Cabell." Galveston Daily News (16 December), p. 20.
The author provides a general appraisal of Cabell's career, finding that he "is assuredly a literary artist if America has ever produced one; and he is a man whom posterity will, in all possibility, be very likely to label a genius."

11 BECHOFFER, CARL ERIC. "James Branch Cabell," in his The Literary Renaissance in America. London: William Heinemann, pp. 42-56.
The author provides an introduction to Cabell's works and a synopsis of Jurgen, concluding that "one feels that the old Puritan order in America must be suffering more from the delightful works of Mr. Cabell than from almost any other of the writers who have dared to enter the list against its traditions."

12 BOYNTON, PERCY H. "Mr. Cabell Expounds Himself." The English Journal, 12 (April), 258-265.
The author provides a general appraisal of Cabell and his works.

13 CANBY, HENRY SEIDEL. Review of The High Place. The Literary Review (15 December), 363.
Concerning this book, "The knowing will find it indecent..., although the naive may read without offence; but the wise will recognize that here in spite of malicious gaiety is a moralizing tale."

14 CHAMBERLIN, IRENE BYRNE. "James Branch Cabell." Chicago Women's Club Bulletin (May), pp. 521-524.
The writer provides an analysis of Cabell and his works.

15 CROWLEY, ALEISTER. "Another Note on Cabell." The Reviewer, 3 (July), 907-914.
The author provides an overview of Cabell's philosophy.

16 DeWIT, AUGUSTA. "Nieuwe Englesche Boeken." Nieuwen Rotterdamsche Courant (15 September).
In discussing the Bodley Head edition of The Cream of the Jest, the reviewer notes that the book is not escape literature; rather, it deals with the perception of beauty in a chaotic world.

17 EDDY, FREDERICK B. Review of The Eagle's Shadow. The Literary Review (15 December), 364.
Regarding this book, the original edition was better because the problem is that "Cabell has tried to make this an authentic part of the Cabellian cycle and it really cannot be done."

18 GARLAND, ROBERT. "Today's Books." Baltimore American (4 December), p. 16.
The High Place "is to be numbered among the best of Cabell."

19 LIGHTFOOT, MRS. JOHN B. A Few Minutes. Richmond, Virginia: Virginia Writers Club.
In these minutes of the proceedings of the meetings of the Virginia Writers Club, numerous mentions of Cabell's attendance, as well as statements attributed to him, appear.

20 M., D. L. Review of The High Place. Boston Evening Transcript Book Section (15 December), p. 8.
In this book, Cabell reveals his view of life to be cynical; however, the book contains a good deal of truth.

21 MAIS, S. P. B. "A New Genius of Letters." London Sunday Express (6 May), p. 7.
Cabell is "By far the most amazing portent in modern America.... His work will live so long as there are men to fall in love with fantasies."

22 MONTGOMERY, RICHARD. "An Affirmation." The New Age (29 November), pp. 54-55.
Cabell is a "romantic enthusiast, and it is as romance that Jurgen will live."

23 MORRIS, LLOYD. "Mr. Cabell Portrays an Ancestor of Jurgen." New York Herald Tribune Book Review (2 December), p. 9.
"In spite of qualities of wit and irony, 'The High Place' ultimately cloys." While reading it, one longs "to take a breath of fresh air and look at life...." Also, Cabell's "decorative obscenity" is objectionable.

24 PRIESTLEY, J. B. Review of The Cream of the Jest. The Mercury, 8 (23 July), 319.
This book is "a much better book than Jurgen."

25 S., H. W. "Cabell in Georgia: The Aristocrat of Literature." Cassell's Weekly (15 December), p. 811.

1923

The author provides a short appreciative comment on Cabell, noting that his early books "showed little promise of the great work that was to come."

26 SHEARING, JOSEPH. "'Jurgen' and the Judges." Cassell's Weekly (27 June), p. 489.
The author traces the publishing history of Jurgen from America to England.

27 STAGG, HUNTER. Review of The High Place. Richmond Times-Dispatch (2 December), 3, p. 9.
This book is "one of those novels the discovery of which will cause the entire country to pronounce James Branch Cabell one of the greatest writers of his time and one of the great writers of all time."

28 STARRET, VINCENT. "James Branch Cabell," in his Buried Caesars. Chicago: Covici-McGee, pp. 87-104.
The author provides a critical appraisal of Cabell's works and career, concluding that "Poe and Cabell are almost the two most distinguished figures in American literature."

29 T., N. "James Branch Cabell: Romancer and Apostle of Disillusion." Aberdeen, Scotland, Press and Journal (14 May), p. 4.
Cabell is a writer who conceives beautiful things and writes of them beautifully.

30 WALKER, HENRY. Review of The High Place. New York Herald Books (2 December), p. 17.
This book is "immensely interesting, but hardly to be dignified as a philosophy of life."

1924 A BOOKS

1 BREGENZER, DON M. and SAMUEL LOVEMAN, eds. A Round Table in Poictesme: A Symposium. Cleveland, Ohio: The Colophon Club, 126 pp.
This volume contains critical articles on Cabell by Ernest Boyd; Don Bregenzer; Samuel Loveman; Frank L. Minarik; Ben Ray Redman; M. P. Mooney; Christopher Morley; Edwin Meade Robinson; Howard Wolf; and H. L. Mencken. The book was occasioned by the editors' feeling that "comparatively little has been done in appreciation of the life-long sacrifice and assiduity of James Branch Cabell to literature." Reprinted 1975.A1.

2 HOLT, GUY. A Bibliography of the Writings of James Branch Cabell. Philadelphia, Pennsylvania: The Centaur Book Shop, 73 pp.
The compiler provides descriptions and notes on Cabell's first editions, along with a list of his contributions to books and periodicals. Selected secondary criticism in books and periodicals is also included.

1924 B SHORTER WRITINGS

1 ANON. "The Lantern." New York Tribune (2 January), p. 14.
The reviewer believes that The High Place was written to force the censor's hand.

2 ANON. "Jurgen the Poet." The New Age (10 January), p. 130.
"In all present-day literature perhaps the two greatest books are Ulysses and Jurgen, for they descend to the roots of human existence."

3 ANON. "Mr. Cabell Defends His Romantic Art." New York Times Book Review (19 October), p. 11.
The reviewer points out that in Straws and Prayer Books Cabell reveals his concepts of an ideal, if imaginary, world.

*4 ANON. "Cabell After 20 Years." Brooklyn Daily Eagle (25 October).
The reviewer praises Cabell as being preeminent among Virginia writers. Unlocatable, except as clipping in author's personal scrapbook.

5 ANON. "A Biographical Epilogue." New York Post Literary Review (29 November), p. 3.
It is pleasing to find that in Straws and Prayer Books Cabell is no longer speaking from behind a mask.

6 BALDWIN, CHARLES C. "James Branch Cabell," in his The Men Who Make Our Novels. New York: Dodd, Mead, pp. 74-88.
The author provides appreciative comments, biographical notes, and quotations from Cabell's works. He concludes that Cabell is "the most distinguished writer in America."

7 BOYD, ERNEST A. "James Branch Cabell," in his Portraits, Real and Imaginary. New York: George H. Doran, pp. 171-174.
The author reminisces about having once met Cabell at a party.

1924

8 BOYD, ERNEST. "Literary Diversions." New York Sun (1 November), p. 7.
After his having written so many novels, Cabell's turn to literary criticism in Straws and Prayer Books is a welcome change.

9 BOYNTON, PERCY H. "Mr. Cabell Expounds Himself," in his Some Contemporary Americans. Chicago: University of Chicago Press, pp. 145-161.
The author provides a general view of Cabell and his works, commenting in particular on his style and subject matter. Reprinted 1940.B1.

10 BROMFIELD, LOUIS. "A Shelf of Recent Books." The Bookman, 60 (December), 492-493.
"There is much subtle and delicious humor in Straws and Prayer Books, not the least of which is to be found in the footnotes."

11 BUTCHER, FANNY. "First Novel." Chicago Tribune (19 January), p. 9.
The reviewer comments on the republication of The Eagle's Shadow, but complains that she cannot understand why Cabell wrote The High Place because it is the Jurgen story all over again.

12 DOUGLAS, A. DONALD. Review of The High Place. The New Republic, 38 (2 April), 157.
The reviewer discovers that The High Place "lies too near the tired earth."

13 F., J. "James Branch Cabell." Time, 4 (24 November), 15.
The reviewer finds that in Straws and Prayer Books Cabell "occupies a lonely and wistful place in American letters."

14 FARRAR, JOHN. "James Branch Cabell," in his The Literary Spot-Light. New York: George H. Doran, pp. 175-184.
The author provides a negative portrayal of Cabell, his works, and his house and personal library.

15 FULLER, HENRY B. "One on a Tower," in The Freeman Book. New York: B. W. Huebsch, pp. 311-315.
Reprint of 1921.B26.

16 FULLER, HENRY B. Review of Straws and Prayer Books. The New Republic, 41 (31 December), 151.
This book proves that Cabell approves of the modern world less and less as time passes.

1924

17 GLASGOW, ELLEN. "Mr. Cabell as a Moralist." New York Herald Tribune Books (2 November), pp. 1-2.
"In 'Straws and Prayer Books' Mr. Cabell...reveals himself again as a moralist and a merrymaker. Not since Voltaire has pessimism worn so gay and gallant a smile." Moreover, the book is "a strange and beautiful volume."

18 GUNTHER, JOHN. "Cabell's Valedictory." Chicago News (26 November), p. 12.
Upon reading Straws and Prayer Books one will find that its author is "a sensitive and intelligent artist," although the book itself is a strange "potpurri."

19 HUNEKER, JOSEPHINE G. Intimate Letters of James Gibbons Huneker. New York: Boni and Liveright, pp. 273-274.
In a letter to John Quinn, Huneker makes passing references to Jurgen, finding it "a clever pasticcio; the shell not the interior glow of both Rabelais and Anatole France."

20 JORDAN-SMITH, PAUL. "James Branch Cabell," in his On Strange Altars. New York: Albert and Charles Boni, pp. 200-213.
In this general critical chapter on Cabell, the author concludes that he is "the Anatole France of America."

21 L., J. W. Review of Beyond Life. Boston Evening Transcript Book Section (16 February), p. 4.
The reviewer offers only oblique impressionistic praise of the book.

22 M., D. L. "Books of the Day." Boston Evening Transcript (31 December), pp. 3, 4.
Straws and Prayer Books is "truly the most diverting" of all of Cabell's works.

23 SCHNITTKIND, HENRY T. "Gulliver Visits James Branch Cabell." The Stratford Monthly (June), pp. 233-239.
The author makes fictional use of Jonathan Swift's Gulliver and of Cabell.

24 STAGG, HUNTER. "The Beautiful Happening." The Reviewer, 4 (January), 147-152.
The author discusses Cabell's statement that he attempts "to write perfectly of beautiful happenings."

25 STALLINGS, LAURENCE. "The First Reader." New York World (16 January), p. 9.
The High Place is "fantastic, as might be expected."

1924

*26 STALLINGS, LAURENCE. "The First Reader." New York World (17 November).
In Straws and Prayer Books the reader will find the best of Cabell's criticism. Unlocatable, except as clipping in author's personal scrapbook.

27 VAN DOREN, CARL. "Irony in Velvet: The Short Stories of James Branch Cabell." The Century Magazine, 108 (August), 561-566.
After discussing the themes found in Cabell's short stories, the author finds that "the temper with which he approaches all these themes is ironic, so much so that he regularly distresses readers who prefer to have their romances entirely romantic."

28 VAN DOREN, CARL. "Hawthorne, Melville, Cabell." The Nation, 119 (29 October), 470.
Judging from Straws and Prayer Books and From the Hidden Way, the reviewer determines that as a writer of romances, Cabell has achieved sufficient stature to be ranked with Nathaniel Hawthorne and Herman Melville.

29 VAN DOREN, CARL. "Two Heroes in Poictesme." The Century Magazine, 119 (November), 129-134.
The writer finds that Jurgen and Figures of Earth are mutually dependent upon each other.

30 VAN DOREN, CARL. "Getting the Ground-Plan of Mr. Cabell's Work." The Literary Digest International Book Review, 3 (December), 12-14.
The author presents an overview of Cabell's world-vision and shows how his books are best approached.

31 WRIGHT, CUTHBERT. "The Best Butter?" The Dial, 76 (April), 361-363.
In writing a tandem review of Jurgen and The High Place, the reviewer notes that Cabell has been overly praised but that nevertheless he is quite good.

1925 A BOOKS

1 BREGENZER, DON. A List of the Cabelliana Belonging to Don Bregenzer of Cleveland. Cleveland, Ohio: Privately Printed.
This unpaged pamphlet is important only because it lists first and subsequent editions, contributions to books and periodicals, and some criticism and other miscellaneous items relating to Cabell.

2 VAN DOREN, CARL. James Branch Cabell. New York: Robert M. McBride, 87 pp.
The author provides a critical appraisal of Cabell's works, to which is appended a list of his books. Reprinted 1932.A2.

3 WALPOLE, HUGH. The Art of James Branch Cabell. New York: Robert M. McBride.
Revised edition of 1920.A2.

1925 B SHORTER WRITINGS

1 ANON. "James Branch Cabell Versus God." Current Opinion, 78 (March), 340.
In this short note on the epilogue of Straws and Prayer Books, the author finds that Cabell has imbedded there his philosophy of life.

2 BUTCHER, FANNY. "Cabell's Latest Hailed." Chicago Tribune (10 January), p. 9.
The reviewer finds that Straws and Prayer Books reflects Cabell's theories of writing.

3 DOWNER, OLIN. "Cabell's 'Jurgen'...." New York Times (20 November), p. 18.
The author provides a news story on the occasion of Deems Taylor's performance of the operatic adaptation of Jurgen.

*4 McNEILL, WARREN A. "Cabell Fills Gap." Richmond Times-Dispatch (25 April).
The Silver Stallion should "delight persons of imagination." Unlocatable, except as clipping in author's personal scrapbook.

5 MACY, JOHN. "American Fiction," in his The Story of the World's Literature. New York: Liveright, Ch. 47.
The author provides brief references to Cabell as a prose stylist.

6 MAINSARD, JOSEPH. "L'Evasion de James Branch Cabell." Les Cahiers du Sud (November), pp. 679-697.
The author draws upon Cabell's novels in order to present his world view.

7 MENCKEN, H. L. "James Branch Cabell," in his Americana. New York: Alfred A. Knopf, p. 301.

In a short discussion of Cabell and his works, the author finds him to be Virginia's "principal living inhabitant."

8 STAGG, HUNTER. "The Absence of Mr. Cabell." Brentano's Book Chat, 4 (March/April), 23-27.
The author provides a short sketch about Cabell's personal elusiveness in Richmond.

9 STEVENSON, BURTON E. "Cabell's Poetry." New York Evening Sun (17 January), p. 7.
The reviewer traces the publishing history of From the Hidden Way and then provides quotations from it.

10 VANCE, J. FRAZIER. "A Pair of Travellers Into Unknown Worlds." Boston Evening Transcript Book Section (31 January), p. 2.
The author provides a comparison between Jonathan Swift's Gulliver and Cabell's Jurgen. Both writers want reform, but Swift finds man an odious animal while Cabell finds that man has been "befooled by a shadow" of his own raising.

11 VAN DOREN, CARL and MARK VAN DOREN. "James Branch Cabell," in their American and British Literature Since 1890. New York: Century, pp. 74-78.
The authors provide an extended discussion of Cabell's plan, intention, and accomplishments in creating and populating his fictional and mythological realm of Poictesme.

1926 A BOOKS--NONE

1926 B SHORTER WRITINGS

1 ANON. Review of The Silver Stallion. The Independent, 119 (26 May), 639.
The reviewer finds the book somewhat tiresome, concluding that "Mr. Cabell has lost the habit of downright, objective story-telling in which he passed his youth so successfully."

2 ANON. Review of The Silver Stallion. The Spectator, 136 (12 June), 1012.
Writing about Cabell's latest book, the reviewer finds of its author that "Talented he certainly is: a brilliant seeker after effects, but not, eminently, wholly an agreeable one."

3 ANON. Review of The Silver Stallion. The Nation and The Athenaeum, 39 (26 June), 362.
The reviewer finds that Cabell's "Americanized mediaevalism must be liked or heartily disliked. That is all.... He has the humor of fantastic pedantry and of calculated and colloquial bathos...."

4 ANON. Review of The Silver Stallion. The Dial, 81 (August), 171.
In a brief mention, the author finds that the book is composed of "ten elegant and silly uproarious books...but not even the most carping can deny the sovereignty of his imagination."

*5 ANON. Review of The Silver Stallion. Saturday Night (28 August).
The reviewer has no regrets that this is Cabell's last book. Unlocatable, except as a clipping in author's personal scrapbook.

6 ANON. Review of The Music From Behind the Moon. The Independent, 117 (25 September), 361.
"With all due respects to Mr. Cabell, the outstanding things about this volume are the eight wood engravings... and the excellence of the bookmaking...."

7 ANON. Review of The Music From Behind the Moon. Boston Evening Transcript (23 October), p. 4.
The reviewer summarizes the plot, concluding that "One misses the gusto of the earlier books."

8 ANON. Review of The Silver Stallion. The Booklist, 23 (November), 78-79.
Plot summary.

9 BALLOU, ROBERT O. "Time Gnaws All." Chicago Daily News (9 June), p. 14.
In The Silver Stallion the reviewer finds that Cabell is becoming saddened with old age.

10 BATES, ERNEST SUTHERLAND. "Mr. Cabell's Problem." The Nation, 122 (19 May), 559-560.
In The Silver Stallion the reviewer finds that on the surface Cabell is a romanticist but beneath he is a classicist.

11 BEACH, JOSEPH WARREN. "James Branch Cabell," in his The Outlook for American Prose. Chicago: University of Chicago Press, pp. 63-80.

1926

The author provides a study of Cabell's prose style, placing it in a historical context.

12 BEACH, JOSEPH WARREN. "Pedantic Study of Two Critics." American Speech, 1 (March), 299-306.
In a discussion of Cabell's and H. L. Mencken's styles the author concludes that the former's style is in the tradition of Thomas DeQuincey. Reprinted 1968.B1.

13 BEACH, JOSEPH WARREN. "The Holy Bottle." The Virginia Quarterly Review, 2 (April), 175-186.
The author provides an overview of Cabell's works.

14 BENSON, ELIZABETH. "A Child's Impression of Lewis, Mencken, Cabell, Arlen, and Other Literary Figures." Vanity Fair (November), pp. 73, 122, 124.
This article, written by a twelve-year old prodigy, finds that Cabell may well be the master of modern American literature. He is "the lone wolf of American letters...." But "perhaps he spun the cobweb of his dreams too fine in The Biography of Manuel."

15 BROUN, HEYWOOD. "It Seems to Me." New York World (27 April), p. 13.
The reviewer admits that, although he does not as a rule care for Cabell's novels, he does like The Silver Stallion.

16 BUTCHER, FANNY. "'The Silver Stallion' is not Cabell." Chicago Tribune (8 May), p. 11.
The reviewer finds that this is not Cabell at his best.

17 CESTRE, C. and B. M. GAGNOT. "James Branch Cabell," in their Anthologie de la Litterature Americaine. Paris: Librairie Delagrave, pp. 275-280.
The authors present a brief biographical sketch of Cabell and reprint chapter 2 of Jurgen.

18 CHAPPELL, NAOMI CASSIDY. Review of The Silver Stallion. Richmond News Leader (23 August), p. 12.
The reviewer praises the book's satire, spectacle, and pageantry.

19 CRAWFORD, JOHN W. "James Branch Cabell Brings Tidings." New York Times Book Review (25 April), p. 2.
Cabell's The Silver Stallion is an exhilarating tonic which is hereby recommended...."

20 DeCASSERES, BENJAMIN. "James Branch Cabell," in his Forty Immortals. New York: Seven Arts, pp. 109-117.
The author provides superficial comments about Cabell and his works.

21 DeCASSERES, BENJAMIN. "Cabell Introduces Cinderella to Mephistopheles." New York Times Book Review (3 October), p. 2.
The reviewer praises the poetry, humor, and laughter in The Music From Behind the Moon.

22 DeCASSERES, BENJAMIN. "Five Portraits on Galvanized Iron: James Branch Cabell." American Mercury, 9 (December), 394-395.
The author provides a brief impressionistic note on Cabell as a writer, concluding that it "may be that Cabell is the Prometheus of an American Renaissance...."

23 DREW, ELIZABETH. The Modern Novel. New York: Harcourt, Brace, passim.
Cabell is mentioned in eight places.

24 J., E. M. "Cabell Continues." Springfield, Massachusetts, Republican (27 June), p. 7.
The reviewer finds The Silver Stallion "very typical" of Cabell's earlier books, but "perhaps there is the added cynicism of growing wisdom and age in it, perhaps a little more extravagances of fancy and of wit...."

25 KRUTCH, JOSEPH WOOD. Review of The Silver Stallion. Saturday Review of Literature, 2 (8 May), 769-770.
From this book, "which reveals no trace of any decline of its author's marvellous fertility of invention," it is "very easy to see that Mr. Cabell's tone and emphasis have been gradually shifted until what was once a romantic faith tinged with irony has become a cynicism...."

26 M., F. J. Review of The Silver Stallion. Catholic World, 123 (August), 712-713.
"The whole book..., while clever and brilliant, is blasphemously offensive. Its whole moral and philosophical tone is degrading...."

27 McCLURE, JOHN. "Literature and Less." New Orleans Times-Picayune (1 August), p. 4.
The author provides a general appraisal of Cabell's works, concluding that "none who pretend to be familiar with contemporary American literature can remain ignorant of the

'Biography,' the most ambitious and the most successful large-scale production of our day."

28 MIMS, EDWIN. "James Branch Cabell," in his The Advancing South. Garden City, New York: Doubleday, Page, passim.
This book contains five unrelated references to Cabell.

29 MOORE, LOUIS. Review of The Silver Stallion. The Literary Digest International Book Review, 4 (June), 451.
The book is "thoroughly typical" of Cabell's works, and its substance "is the Manuel legend."

30 NEWMAN, FRANCES. "Tales of Romance." The Bookman, 63 (June), 481.
No one need try to understand The Silver Stallion "unless he has read and understood Jurgen and Figures of Earth...."

31 PATERSON, ISABEL. "Dominion and Dreams." New York Herald Tribune Books (9 May), pp. 1, 2.
In The Silver Stallion Cabell "supplies the consolation of laughter under the undeceiving mask of romance."

32 PAYNE, LEONIDAS WARREN, JR. "James Branch Cabell," in his Selections From American Literature: Later American Writers, Part Two. Chicago: Rand McNally, pp. 898-899.
The author reprints Cabell's "Porcelain Cups" and includes a brief biographical and critical introduction to the author.

33 RAMON. "James Branch Cabell." Queensland, Australia, Morning Bulletin (16 April), p. 3.
The author provides a general article on Cabell, concluding that "Those who have the key to the world of Cabell can enter a strange world of fantasy where reason does not destroy romance, and where one may discover again and again something new and beautiful."

34 S., H. Review of The Music From Behind the Moon. New York World Book World (5 September), p. 4.
"That it will add a cubit to Cabell's stature we doubt. There is not a new note in it. The book is presented as a collector's item rather than as a contribution to contemporary literature."

*35 SALPETER, HARRY. "The First Reader." New York World (26 April).
"The Silver Stallion is as good as Jurgen; if not better." Unlocatable, except as a clipping in the author's personal scrapbook.

36 SCHRIFTGIESSER, EDWARD B. Review of The Silver Stallion. Boston Evening Transcript Book Section (1 May), p. 2.
This book is further proof that Cabell does not seek to avoid the realities of life.

37 SCHRIFTGIESSER, EDWARD B. "The Symbolic Philosophy of Poictesme's King." Boston Evening Transcript (21 August), pp. 1, 3.
Cabell is an author who writes for those who are unafraid of life as well as those who are not too well satisfied with it.

38 SHIPLEY, JOSEPH. Review of The Silver Stallion. Literary Review, 6 (15 May), 3.
Like other books about the Fellowship of the Silver Stallion, the present one "preserves that power to delight which more continuously characterized other sections of the saga."

39 STAGG, HUNTER. "Cabell Tells an Old Tale." Richmond Times-Dispatch (26 September), 3, p. 16.
In a review of The Music From Behind the Moon, the writer praises Cabell's simplicity and beauty.

40 VAN DOREN, CARL. Review of The Music From Behind the Moon. New York Herald Tribune Books (14 November), p. 2.
"It is...the essence of Cabell."

41 W., D. B. Review of The Silver Stallion. The New Republic, 47 (4 August), 317.
"For purest savoring" it should be read "immediately after a novel or two by Archibald Marshall."

42 W., D. B. Review of The Music From Behind the Moon. The New Republic, 48 (22 September), 128.
The book is "an artistic achievement for publisher as well as author."

1927 A BOOKS

1 MENCKEN, H. L. James Branch Cabell. New York: Robert M. McBride. Large paper edition misdated 1928; small paper edition properly dated 1927; issued simultaneously.
In this thirty-one-page pamphlet the author provides a general critical appraisal of Cabell, with a list of his books. He concludes that in Cabell there is "more assurance of permanence than in any other contemporary American of his trade." Reprinted 1967.B18.

1927

2 WALL, BERNHARDT. A Visit to James Branch Cabell. Lime Rock, Connecticut: Privately Printed, unpaged (four leaves).
The author reports on a private visit to Cabell.

1927 B SHORTER WRITINGS

1 ANDREWS, O. B., JR. "In 'Something About Eve' Are to be Found Cabellian Qualities of Wit, Charm, Irony." Columbus, Georgia, Enquirer Sun (4 December), p. 8.
"The works of James Branch Cabell present a strange galaxy to the average American eye and intellect. The eye can discern no sense in them and the intellect can conjure up no possible moral purpose or sound advice to be found in his satire."

2 BLEI, FRANZ. "James Branch Cabell." Die Literarische Welt, 3 (14 October), 315.
The author describes his first encounter with Cabell's works and gives a brief overview of them.

3 BOLANDER, CARL AUGUST. "Historiografen i Poictesme." Dagens Nyheter (Stockholm) (7 September), A, p. 7.
In reviewing the Bodley Head edition of Straws and Prayer Books, the reviewer provides an overview of Cabell's previous novels.

4 CANBY, HENRY SEIDEL. Review of Something About Eve. Saturday Review of Literature, 4 (29 October), 1-2.
The reviewer recounts Cabell's fictional methods and his contribution to literature, but he finds that Cabell's art suffers because of his romantic idealism.

5 CROFT-COOKE, RUPERT. "James Branch Cabell." The Reader (London), 3 (November), 54-57.
The author provides a general appraisal of Cabell's works, noting his "rather hopeless philosophy."

*6 EMANUEL, JAY. "Something About James Branch Cabell." Brooklyn Citizen (4 December).
In reviewing Something About Eve, the writer praises Cabell's ability to carve "out a niche for Man in a world that is Woman's...." Unlocatable, except as a clipping in the author's personal scrapbook.

*7 GARRETT, M. H. "Cabell and His Magic." St. Joseph Gazette (13 November).
Unlocatable, cited in Brewer, 1957.A1.

8 HAZARD, LUCY LOCKWOOD. "Escape to Poictesme," in her The Frontier in American Literature. New York: Thomas Y. Crowell, pp. 83-87.
The author compares Edgar Allan Poe and Cabell as Southern Romanticists. She finds Cabell in revolt against modern Realism.

9 HUTCHINSON, PERCY. "Something, But Not a Great Deal, About Eve." New York Times Book Review (25 September), p. 2.
The reviewer, writing about Something About Eve, finds Cabell unique among modern writers.

10 KARSNER, DAVID. "Censored Into Fame." New York Herald Tribune Magazine (24 July), pp. 12, 13, 31.
The author provides an extended appraisal of Cabell's career, with numerous citations to and quotations from his works.

11 KELLOGG, ELENORE. "James Branch Cabell is Happy Though Ignored in Richmond." New York World (20 November), M, p. 5.
An interview.

12 NILES, ABBE. "Feats of Fancy." The Nation, 124 (5 January), 18.
In reviewing The Music From Behind the Moon, the writer praises Cabell's allegory, philosophy, and craftsmanship.

*13 R., N. L. "James Branch Cabell." Brisbane, Australia, Courier (3 September).
Unlocatable, cited in Brewer, 1957.A1.

14 RASCOE, BURTON. "Some Several Literary Offerings." The Bookman, 66 (October), 211-213.
Something About Eve "is enough to make other scribblers wish to chuck writing in despair forever."

15 ROBERTSON, WILLIAM J. "James Branch Cabell," in his The Changing South. New York: Boni and Liveright, pp. 224-226.
Cabell is "probably the South's leading writer,...but the ordinary business man in the South would suffer from a cracking of the brain if he would attempt to comprehend the subtleties of Jurgen...."

16 S., A. "James Branch Cabel" [sic]. Cape Town, South Africa, Cape Argus (17 January), p. 6.
Fed on "deliberate illusions," the reader "cannot help but be nervous that the whole of his literary theory may be likewise one more illusion born of Cabell's brain for his

own diversion.... The fault with Cabell is that he is drunk with his freedom."

17 SINCLAIR, UPTON. "The Charm-Poacher," in his Money Writes. New York: Albert and Charles Boni, pp. 100-103.
The author provides a negative appraisal of Cabell, finding Jurgen as deadly and dangerous as a rattlesnake.

*18 SPENCER, JAMES B. "Signed by Mr. Cabell." The Archive (October).
Unlocatable, cited in Brewer, 1957.A1.

19 STRODE, HUDSON. "Mr. Cabell Lays by His Fig-Leaf." The New Republic, 53 (30 November), 52.
In reviewing Something About Eve, the writer finds that Cabell has become mellow and with the mellowness "has come a new simplicity of expression...."

20 VAN DOREN, CARL. "A Call for a Commentator." The Nation, 125 (12 October), 386.
In reviewing Something About Eve, the writer takes the occasion to call for more interpretative criticism of Cabell's works.

1928 A BOOKS

1 COVER, JAMES P. Notes On Jurgen. New York: Robert M. McBride, 115 pp.
The author provides sources and analogues for Jurgen.

2 McNEIL, WARREN A. Cabellian Harmonics. New York: Random House, 103 pp.
The author provides an interpretation of Cabell's schema, especially as dramatized in the Biography of Manuel.

1928 B SHORTER WRITINGS

1 ANON. "Rascoe, Springs Guests of Cabell." Richmond News Leader (2 June), p. 14.
The author provides a news story centering on the visit.

2 ANON. "James Branch Cabell." Glasgow, Scotland, Herald (19 July), p. 7.
The author provides an overall appraisal of Cabell's works, finding that he "is one who has shed all the illusions that engage the successive stages of man's life, even

to the last and most pathetic illusion of one's own supreme importance...."

*3 ANON. "The Mystery of Mr. J. B. Cabell." Yorkshire, England, Post (24 December).
Unlocatable, cited in Brewer, 1957.A1.

4 ANON. Review of The White Robe. New York Times Book Review (30 December), p. 12.
The reviewer finds the book derivative of Jorns-Karl Huysman's La-Bas.

5 CLARK, EMILY. "Eve and Mr. Cabell: and the Archbishop." The Virginia Quarterly Review, 4 (January), 114-117.
The reviewer finds Cabell's Something About Eve the most beautiful of his books.

6 ELIAS, I. H. "Three Gentlemen--A Glimpse." The Periwig (February), pp. 25-30.
Writing of Cabell, H. L. Mencken, and Thomas Beer, the author provides general comments on Cabell works, especially the suppression of Jurgen.

7 ERNST, MORRIS L. and WILLIAM SEAGLE. To the Pure. New York: Viking, passim.
The authors make several passing references to the censorship of Jurgen.

8 HERGESHEIMER, JOSEPH. "James Branch Cabell." The American Mercury, 13 (January), 38-47.
The author provides an overview of Cabell, his technique, myth-making, and achievement in contemporary letters.

9 KARSNER, DAVID. "James Branch Cabell," in his Sixteen Authors to One. New York: Lewis Copeland, pp. 27-41.
This chapter on Cabell centers on an interview conducted with him.

10 McCARDELL, ROY L. "Mr. Wogglebaum Cooks an Opera." The Bookman, 66 (February), 637-639.
The author makes dramatic comic use of Jurgen.

11 MARBLE, ANNIE RUSSELL. "James Branch Cabell," in her Study of the Modern Novel. New York: D. Appleton, pp. 274-281.
The author provides an overview of Cabell's works, with synopses of several of his books, concluding that he has influenced a number of other writers.

1928

12 MENCKEN, H. L. "Review of The Storisende Edition." The American Mercury, 14 (June), 251-253.
The reviewer traces Cabell's rise to literary fame, and comments on the new edition, along with its prefaces and illustrations.

13 MICHAUD, RÉGIS. "James Branch Cabell and the Escape to Poictesme," in his The American Novel To-day. Boston: Little Brown, pp. 200-237.
The author discusses Cabell's important contributions to American Romanticism and offers a summary of his "ironistic philosophy."

14 MORE, PAUL ELMER. "James Branch Cabell," in The Demon of the Absolute: New Shelburne Essays I. Princeton, New Jersey: Princeton University Press, pp. 58-63.
The author provides a general appraisal of Cabell and his works, placing him in the category of the "aesthetes."

15 MORE, PAUL ELMER. "The Modern Current in American Literature." The Forum, 79 (January), 127-136.
The author provides an overview of Cabell and of a number of other contemporary novelists.

16 MUNSON, GORHAM B. "The Quality of Readability." The Bookman, 68 (November), 335-338.
The reviewer finds The White Robe to be "the essence of sophomoric 'wisdom.'"

17 RASCOE, BURTON. "Contemporary Reminiscences: Cabell and Glasgow." Arts and Decoration (November), p. 98.
The author provides a report of a visit to Cabell at his home in Richmond, at which time he commented on his work and the demolition of the house in which he was born.

18 RICHARDSON, EUDORA RAMSAY. "Richmond and Its Writers." The Bookman, 68 (December), 449-453.
The author provides humorous comments on Cabell as a Richmonder.

1929 A BOOKS

1 CRANWELL, JOHN PHILIPS and JAMES P. COVER. Notes on Figures of Earth. New York: Robert M. McBride, 140 pp.
"It was with the purpose of helping the readers of Figures of Earth...that this book was prepared."

1929 B SHORTER WRITINGS

1 ANON. Stadium Concerts Review: A Publication of the College of the City of New York, 12 (August), 25.
Deems Taylor is quoted regarding his musical adaptation of Jurgen.

2 BROWN, LEONARD, ed. Modern American and British Short Stories. New York: Harcourt Brace, pp. 80-96.
The editor reprints Cabell's "A Brown Woman" from The Certain Hour and makes a brief mention of Cabell and his place in fiction.

3 BRYAN, JOSEPH III. "James Branch Cabell Writes Finis to Notable Book Series." Richmond News Leader (30 October), p. 14.
The Way of Ecben "is an anguish to a reviewer, whom it lures necessarily headlong on a treacherous course...." This is owing to the fact that "Mr. Cabell's anagrams and allegories are seldom obvious."

4 CANBY, HENRY SEIDEL. "James Branch Cabell," in his American Estimates. New York: Harcourt, Brace, pp. 70-79.
The author provides a short overview of Cabell's works, suggesting that he is somewhat too erotic in them.

5 CLARK, EMILY. "The Case of Mr. Cabell vs. the Author of the Biography." The Virginia Quarterly Review, 5 (July), 336-345.
The author recounts Cabell's part in the founding of The Reviewer and also comments on him personally.

6 CLARKE, ALAN BURTON. "James Branch Cabell Brings the Poictesme 'Biography' to a Close." Richmond Times-Dispatch (27 October), 2, p. 1.
The author provides a general appraisal of the Biography of Manuel.

7 GUERARD, ALBERT. "Art for Art's Sake: Cabellism." New York Herald Tribune Books (9 June), pp. 1, 5, 6.
The writer provides a discussion of Cabell's theories of beauty.

8 HANSEN, HARRY. "Cabell Reviews his Reviewers." New York World (31 March), M, p. 10.
The author reviews Cabell's attitudes toward those who have reviewed his books and finds that he "may never have been a success commercially, but as a writer his battle was won years ago."

1929

9 HART, THEODORE. "No Possible Doubt." Macon, Georgia, News (21 April), p. 4.
The author defends Cabell against the charge that he is obscure, has bad taste, and has a tendency to write platitudes, as well as being adolescent. Cabell is "America's most considerable contribution to the world's literature."

10 HOOKER, EDWARD NILES. "Something About Cabell." The Sewanee Review, 37 (April), 193-203.
The author provides a general critical article on Cabell and his works.

11 KRONENBERGER, LOUIS. "Mr. Cabell Bids Farewell to the Land of Poictesme." New York Times Book Review (27 October), p. 2.
The Way of Ecben "has the merit of a well-told and richly written fable...and the merit of an urbane irony confined to generalities."

12 LUTZ, MARK. "Last Volume of Biography From Cabell Pen Finished." Richmond News Leader (21 October), p. 17.
The author interviews Cabell upon the occasion.

13 McCOLE, CAMILLE, "Something About Cabell." Catholic World, 134 (July), 460-464.
The author provides a general appraisal of Cabell's works, finding that "the work itself is not great." When we read him we want "to escape to a purer realm of literature. And we won't come back."

14 McCORMICK, ELSIE. "A Piece of Her Mind." New York World (20 November), 1, p. 13.
The author provides an article on the occasion of Cabell's announcement that he will write no more. She argues with his dramatization of women.

15 METCALF, JOHN CALVIN. "Twentieth Century Virginia Literature." Richmond News Leader (9 April), pp. 1, 7.
The author provides brief comments on Cabell, included among those of other Virginia writers.

16 MEYER, GERARD PREVIN. "Young Jurgen." The Morningside [an independent literary magazine published by Columbia College of New York City] (August), pp. 16-21.
The author provides a parody of Cabell's literary style.

17 NEWMAN, FRANCES. Frances Newman's Letters. Edited by Hansell Baugh. New York: Horace Liveright, passim.
The volume contains numerous letters exchanged between Miss Newman and Cabell.

18 PALMER, JOE H. "James Branch Cabell: Dualist." Letters, 2 (February), 6-14.

The author provides an overview of Cabell's works in light of his ideas of the three modes of existence--chivalry, gallantry, and poetry.

19 POWYS, JOHN COWPER. The Meaning of Culture. New York: W. W. Norton, 218 pp.

In speaking of the "clever, modern aesthetes," the author notes that he is "not of course referring to Oscar Wilde or James Branch Cabell."

20 RASCOE, BURTON. The Bookman's Daybook. New York: Horace Liveright, passim.

The author records the meeting of Frances Newman and Cabell; lists authors who have imitated Cabell's style; comments on Cabell's work day and his methods of revisions.

21 STAGG, HUNTER. "The Nationality of James Branch Cabell." Richmond [the magazine of the Richmond Chamber of Commerce], 15 (April), 9, 28, 34.

The author finds that Cabell is often considered not to be an American writer because of his subject matter, but Cabell writes as he does because he is an American.

22 VAN DOREN, CARL. "The Afternoon of a Werewolf." New York Herald Tribune Books (6 January), p. 3.

The reviewer finds The White Robe to be the parable of the wolf in sheep's clothing.

23 WICKHAM, HARVEY. "James Branch Cabell," in his The Impuritans. New York: Lincoln MacVegh--Dial Press, pp. 137-168.

The author provides a general discussion and appraisal of Cabell's life and works, noting the way that Cabell, among others, has abandoned the Puritan ethic.

24 ZANDER, ROBERT. "Seeing James Branch Cabell." The Spur, 44 (15 August), 36, 100.

The author reports on an interview with Cabell, finding him elusive and difficult to approach.

1930 A BOOKS--NONE

1930

1930 B SHORTER WRITINGS

*1 ANON. "Brother Cabell." The News. Alpha Zeta Chapter of the Kappa Alpha Order, Williamsburg, Virginia (May, 1930).
Unlocatable, except as note in author's personal scrapbook.

2 BABB, STANLEY E. "Mrs. James Branch Cabell Relates of the Life of Her Famed Author Husband." Galveston, Texas, News (6 March), p. 13.
Mrs. Cabell reveals much about the work habits of her husband in this interview.

3 BEACH, JOSEPH WARREN. "The Decade of the Doomed." The Nation, 131 (3 December), 622.
While reviewing Some of Us, the reviewer takes the occasion to expound on Cabell's theories of art.

4 BRUNS, FREDERICK. "James Branch Cabell," in his Die Amerikanische Dichtung Der Gegenwart. Leipzig and Berlin: B. G. Teubner, pp. 48-54.
The author discusses Cabell as a modern day romantic ironist and as a satirist.

5 CLARK, EMILY. "Farewell to Youth." Saturday Review of Literature, 6 (15 February), 733.
Cabell's The Way of Ecben is in complete harmony with the other books in the Storisende Edition.

6 DeCASSERES, BENJAMIN. "Trois Modes d'Evasion Spirituelle." Mercure de France (15 August), pp. 5-17.
The author provides a discussion of Miguel Cervantes, Theophile Gautier, and Cabell. In the section on Cabell he presents an overview of that author's work and philosophy.

7 GLASGOW, ELLEN. "The Biography of Manuel." Saturday Review of Literature (7 June), pp. 1108-1110.
"There is little hazard in the repeated assertion that Mr. Cabell is already a classic.... His books will probably survive many changing fashions in literature.... Almost alone among American authors he has dared to look into the encompassing void and to laugh because it is bottomless."

8 KRONENBERGER, LOUIS. "Mr. Cabell Records His Enthusiasms." New York Times Book Review (21 December), p. 2.
The reviewer finds Some of Us to be an "appreciative survey" of the literati of the 1920s.

9 McINTYRE, CLARA F. "Mr. Cabell's Cosmos." <u>The Sewanee Review</u>, 38 (July-September), 278-285.

The author provides an overview of Cabell's world vision. She finds that for Cabell, "Life, for the rare and for the individual, is a series of apparently meaningless repetitions."

10 PARRINGTON, VERNON LOUIS. "The Incomparable Mr. Cabell," in his <u>Beginnings of Critical Realism in America</u>. New York: Harcourt, Brace.

Reprint of 1921.B41.

11 PARRINGTON, VERNON LOUIS. "The Incomparable Mr. Cabell," in his <u>Main Currents in American Thought</u>. New York: Harcourt, Brace. Volume 3.

Reprint of 1921.B41.

12 PATERSON, ISABEL. "Thus It Was in the Old Days." New York <u>Herald Tribune Books</u> (6 April), pp. 1, 6.

In writing about the Storisende Edition, the author praises Cabell's dream world and his life's accomplishment.

13 PATTEE, FRED LEWIS. "James Branch Cabell," in his <u>The New American Literature, 1890-1930</u>. New York: Century, pp. 350-355.

The author finds that Cabell "has worked out a unique mythology with personages as <u>sui generis</u> as if from the newly discovered record of a lost generation." Reprinted 1968.B14.

14 PRUETTE, LORINE. "Horvendile-Cabell." New York <u>Herald Tribune Books</u> (16 November), pp. 3, 4.

In reviewing <u>Some of Us</u> the reviewer is "beguiled" by the way Cabell says things rather than by what he actually says.

15 R., F. L. Review of <u>Some of Us</u>. <u>The Outlook</u>, 156 (29 October), 347.

The reviewer finds this collection of essays better than Cabell's other books.

16 RAMOS, J. A. "James Branch Cabell." <u>Revista de la Habana</u> (Havana, Cuba), 4 (October), 1-11.

The author provides a general appraisal of Cabell's works, regarding him as a romantic, fantastic writer, a gentleman and a dreamer who has achieved success in a pragmatic world.

1930

17 RICHARDSON, EUDORA RAMSAY. "The South Grows Up." The Bookman, 70 (January), 545-550.

The writer provides a general article on the rebirth of Southern literature, finding that if "the South had produced only James Branch Cabell, the immensity of its contribution to letters would leave the rest of America in its debt."

18 TATE, ALLEN. "Mr. Cabell's Farewell." The New Republic, 111 (8 January), 201-202.

While reviewing The Way of Ecben, the reviewer takes the occasion to do a revaluation of Cabell's contribution to literature, suggesting that some of Cabell's books will have a lasting place in the literature of America.

1931 A BOOKS

1 HORAN, THOMAS, ed. The Romaunt of Manuel Pig-Tender. Dalton, Georgia: Postprandial Press.

This short poem centers on the origins of the Dom Manuel legend.

1931 B SHORTER WRITINGS

1 ALLEN, GAY WILSON. "Jurgen and Faust." The Sewanee Review, 39 (October-December), 485-492.

The author identifies and discusses the similarities between Cabell's Jurgen and Goethe's Faust.

2 ANON. Review of Domnei. New York Times Book Review (18 January), p. 17.

The reviewer speculates that Cabell will "occupy a considerable place in the literary histories" of the future.

3 ANON. "Noted Authors to be Guests of University." Richmond Times-Dispatch (19 October), p. 10.

In a general story about the Southern Writers' Conference to be held in Charlottesville, Virginia, the writer mentions that Cabell is one of those who have been invited.

4 ANON. "Southern Authors Informally Swap Views at University." Richmond Times-Dispatch (24 October), p. 11.

In reporting on the Southern Writers' Conference at Charlottesville, Virginia, the writer mentions Cabell's presence.

1931

5 BLANKENSHIP, RUSSELL. "James Branch Cabell," in his American Literature. New York: Henry Holt, pp. 685-695.
After discussing Cabell as a romancer, the author considers each of his works and then places him in the context of modern letters. He concludes that "Cabell is not popular. Frankly, he is simply too good for most readers."

6 CLARK, EMILY. Innocence Abroad. New York: Alfred A. Knopf, pp. 35-52.
This book, which relates the story of the founding of The Reviewer, contains myriad references to Cabell and to Richmond life and letters during the 1920s.

7 CLARKE, ALAN BURTON. "On Not Reading James Branch Cabell." Richmond Times-Dispatch (1 March), 2, p. 3.
The author provides a news story on an article about Cabell in the current issue of The Bookman.

8 COLTON, A. "Critics of Different Species." Saturday Review of Literature, 7 (24 January), 548.
In reviewing Some of Us, the writer finds that "Mr. Cabell writes noticeably good English when his attitudes and neologies are not too obsessional."

9 CURRIE, BARTON. "James Branch Cabell," in his Fishers of Books. Boston: Little, Brown, pp. 274, 310, 311, 312.
The author provides assorted notes for those interested in Cabell's books.

10 ELGSTROM, A. L. "James Branch Cabell: Romantik kontra Puritanism." Svenska Dagbladet (Stockholm) (4 January), p. 2.
The author provides an overview of Cabell's works.

11 HATCHER, HARLAN. "On Not Having Read James Branch Cabell." The Bookman, 72 (February), 597-599.
The author confesses that he has not read Cabell because "I have failed to find convincing evidence of the creative genius with which Mr. Cabell is charged."

12 McNEILL, WARREN A. "Great Virginians: James Branch Cabell." Richmond Times-Dispatch (29 March), p. 7.
One in a series of articles, this piece centers on Cabell and his works.

13 MEADE, J. R. "Cabell Returns to Earth." New York Herald Tribune Books (19 July), p. 11.

1931

The author conducts a personal interview in which Cabell talks about writing, writers, personal matters, and Richmond.

14 PINCKNEY, JOSEPHINE. "Southern Writers' Conference." Saturday Review of Literature, 8 (7 November), 266.
The author makes passing references to Cabell's presence at the event.

15 TANTE, DILLY ("STANLEY KUNITZ"). "James Branch Cabell," in his Living Authors. New York: H. W. Wilson, pp. 61-62.
The author provides a short biographical sketch of Cabell.

1932 A BOOKS

1 BRUSSEL, I. R. A Bibliography of the Writings of James Branch Cabell. Philadelphia: Centaur Book Shop, 126 pp.
The compiler provides collations and notations on Cabell's first editions, along with his contributions to books and periodicals. Included also is secondary criticism in books, pamphlets, and periodicals.

2 VAN DOREN, CARL. James Branch Cabell. New York: Literary Guild, 87 pp.
Reprint of 1925.A2.

1932 B SHORTER WRITINGS

1 ANGLY, EDWARD. "Cabell Deserts Silver Stallion for Dusty Car." New York Herald Tribune (4 February), p. 15.
The author provides an interview with Cabell.

2 ANON. "Cabell Puts Style Before Idea in a Book." New York Times (4 February), p. 19.
The author provides an interview with Cabell.

3 ANON. "Cabell's Newest Book Released." Richmond News Leader (4 February), p. 3.
The author provides a news story on the release of These Restless Heads.

4 ANON. "Cabell Editor in New Publication." Richmond News Leader (13 September), p. 9.
The author provides a news story on Cabell's becoming an editor of The American Spectator.

5 ANON. "Richmond Snubbed in Sale of Cabell's Newspaper." Richmond News Leader (21 October), p. 28.
The author provides a news story centering on the unavailability of The American Spectator in Richmond.

6 ARVIN, NEWTON. "High in the Brisk Air." The New Republic, 120 (2 March), 78-79.
In reviewing These Restless Heads the writer suggests that Cabell is "a grossly over estimated third-rate Anatole France...."

7 BEACH, JOSEPH WARREN. "Hors d'Oeuvres: Cabell," in his The Twentieth Century Novel. New York: Appleton, Century Crofts, pp. 85-93.
The author provides a general view of Cabell, noting that in all his works "we feel the alternating pulse of dream and disillusion...."

8 BRITT, GEORGE. "Cabell Doesn't Hope to Say Anything New." New York World-Telegram (4 February), p. 30.
The author provides an interview in which Cabell talks about his writing and its influences. Cabell notes here that Burton Rascoe discovered him.

9 CABELL, [JAMES] BRANCH. "Objections to James Branch Cabell." Richmond Times-Dispatch (31 January), 3, p. 6.
Cabell reviews These Restless Heads in a style and manner meant to parody the prose of his critics.

10 DAVENPORT, B. "The Two Mr. Cabells." Saturday Review of Literature, 8 (13 February), 521.
The reviewer finds These Restless Heads to be considerably inferior to Cabell's earlier works published under his full name James Branch Cabell, rather than Branch Cabell.

11 DAVIDSON, DONALD. "A Meeting of Southern Writers." The Bookman, 74 (February), 494-497.
The author makes reference to Cabell's having attended the meeting.

12 DICKINSON, THOMAS H. "James Branch Cabell," in his The Making of American Literature. New York: Appleton, Century, pp. 673-674.
The author provides a brief introduction to Cabell and his works, asserting that he is "a romanticist and an aristocrat who still has a clear set of ideas of the world around him."

1932

13 GLASGOW, ELLEN. "Recent Books I Have Liked." New York Herald Tribune Books (4 December), p. 8.
In a general article about contemporary publishing, the author mentions having liked Cabell's These Restless Heads.

14 HANSEN, HARRY. "The First Reader." New York World Telegram (4 February), p. 23.
"Mr. Cabell...seems to be the only writer who can say the same thing in twenty volumes." In These Restless Heads he "reveals his unchanging intention never to get too serious about human ways...."

15 KRONENBERGER, LOUIS. "Mr. Cabell Suffers No Sea-Change." New York Times Book Review (7 February), p. 2.
Writing of Cabell's achievement in These Restless Heads, the reviewer asserts that "Nobody can dress up the truisms of romance better than he...."

16 LEWISHON, LUDWIG. "James Branch Cabell," in his Expression in America. New York: Harper and Brothers, pp. 194, 530-531.
The author finds that Cabell never progressed with the literary history of the country. "The fields of earth are on fire under our feet," he contends, "and Cabell offers us the day-dreams of a romantic adolescent; there is famine and he goes about hawking expensive and soon cloying sweets."

17 LUTZ, MARK. "Cabell Reflects Lightly." Richmond News Leader (12 February), p. 8.
The reviewer finds that These Restless Heads was "written with great flexibility...of style and mind."

18 McNEILL, WARREN A. "Branch Cabell Leaves James B. to His Past." Richmond Times-Dispatch (17 January), 3, p. 6.
The author provides an interview with Cabell upon the occasion of his dropping the use of his first name.

19 MACY, JOHN. "Cabell New and Old." The Nation, 134 (24 February), 232-233.
The reviewer remarks on the beauty of These Restless Heads.

20 MENCKEN, H. L. "James Branch Cabell." Wings, 6 (February), 5-7.
Speaking of Cabell, the author asserts that "What he tries to do is to construct a world that shall be better than the world of everyday."

21 PARKER, WILLIAM R. "A Key to Cabell." The English Journal, 21 (June), 431-440.
The author provides a brief overview of Cabell's books and ideas.

22 RASCOE, BURTON. "Mr. Cabell of Richmond, Va." Wings, 6 (February), 14-16.
The author provides a brief sketch of Cabell and his works.

23 SEINFEL, RUTH. "Fair Helen is Just a Woman in a Book." New York Evening Post (4 February), p. 8.
This interview contains a number of personal glimpses as revealed by Cabell's wife.

24 SHERWIN, LOUIS. "Ex-Reporter Cabell's Fear of Scribes is Cream of Jest." New York Evening Post (4 February), p. 6.
The author finds that Cabell is a man who dreads publicity, especially interviews, and handles himself poorly before the New York newspapermen.

25 VAN DOREN, CARL. Review of These Restless Heads. Wings, 6 (February), 9-10.
The author describes the Literary Guild's reissue of the book.

26 WARREN, ALBERT. "Leaving Romantic James Behind, Branch Cabell Appears As Realist." Richmond Times-Dispatch (7 February), 3, p. 6.
While reviewing These Restless Heads, the writer finds that Cabell has not changed much over the years.

1933 A BOOKS--NONE

1933 B SHORTER WRITINGS

1 ANON. "Unposted Letters of James Branch Cabell." New York Times Book Review (9 April), p. 9.
Cabell's Special Delivery is a "jolly fabrication."

2 ANON. "One of Cabell's 'Specials' Gets Answered." Richmond Times-Dispatch (18 June), 3, p. 6.
A newspaper reporter sarcastically answers one of the letters in Special Delivery.

1933

3 EDGAR, PELHAM. "Two Anti-Realists: Willa Cather and Cabell," in his The Art of the Novel: From 1700 to the Present Time. New York: Macmillan, pp. 261-267.
The author discusses a number of Cabell's books. He finds Cabell unique in American letters and finds Jurgen to be his best work. Reprinted 1965.B3.

4 FADIMAN, CLIFTON. "James Branch Cabell." The Nation, 136 (12 April), 409-410.
The author provides a discussion of Cabell's views on art and religion.

5 GREBANIER, BERNARD. "Branch Cabell: An Obituary Memoir." Contempo, 4 (5 April), 7-8.
The author deplores Cabell's books since he began writing under the name Branch Cabell.

6 HICKS, GRANVILLE. "James Branch Cabell," in his The Great Tradition. New York: Macmillan, pp. 220-221 and passim.
Cabell has "converted his petulant disgust into a melodramatic pessimism.... He is a fraud,...a sleek smug egoist.... Fortunately few writers have followed the example of Cabell...."

7 LE BRETON, MAURICE. "James Branch Cabell, romancier." Revue Anglo-Américaine, 11 (December-January 1934), 112-128.
Part one of an extended discussion of the Storisende Edition. See 1934.B11.

8 McNEILL, WARREN A. "The Autobiography of a Shy Man." Westminster Magazine, 22 (Summer), 71-76.
The author finds that by adopting the name "Branch Cabell," Cabell is actually beginning an autobiographical phase in his writing career.

9 NABESHIMA, N. "On James Branch Cabell." Studies in English Literature, 13: 365-379.
The author places Cabell in the context of nineteenth and twentieth century American literature, then, relying on primary and secondary sources, goes on to discuss his entire canon.

10 POLLAK, VALENTIN. "James Branch Cabell." Die Literatur, 35 (March), 323-325.
The author provides an introduction to Cabell and an overview of his works.

11 PRUETTE, LORINE. "Mr. Cabell Replies to Letter Writing Pests." New York Herald Tribune Books (26 March), p. 4.
Special Delivery is a book "about a man who doesn't suffer fools gladly" but who is constrained "to suffer them."

12 RASCOE, BURTON. "James Branch Cabell," in his Prometheans. New York: G. P. Putnam's Sons, pp. 273-287.
Amid assorted biographical jottings about Cabell, the author discusses his work in general and the unity of the Biography of Manuel in particular.

13 SCHRIFTGIESSER, EDWARD B. Review of Special Delivery. Boston Evening Transcript (6 May), p. 1.
The book is "a very pleasant collection of light essays."

14 TUCKER, HARRY. "Main Street." Richmond Times-Dispatch (20 March), p. 7.
The author chides Cabell for speaking out against Virginians in the current issue of The Bookman.

15 WARREN, ALBERT. "Open Letter to Mr. Cabell After Reading 'Special Delivery.'" Richmond Times-Dispatch (2 April), 5, p. 7.
The book might have been called Prejudices had not H. L. Mencken preempted the title. "All these replies are eminently readable and generally entertaining."

1934 A BOOKS--NONE

1934 B SHORTER WRITINGS

1 ANON. "Local Author Scores Hit." Richmond Times-Dispatch (4 April), p. 8.
The author discusses Cabell's aversion to the newspaper world.

2 ANON. Review of Ladies and Gentlemen. Saturday Review of Literature, 11 (24 November), 307.
"It is an astonishing and a melancholy thing that any man should wish to present himself to the world in such a character" as he does here as letter writer.

3 ANON. "The Two Truths." Walhalla, North Dakota Mountaineer (6 December), p. 2.
The author provides a philosophical discussion of Cabell's idea that there are but two truths available to man: life and death.

1934

4 CLARK, EMILY. "Branch Cabell's Dream." The Virginia Quarterly Review, 10 (April), 287-290.
The reviewer discusses the dream world of Smirt, concluding that Cabell's place in literature is secure.

5 EVANS, A. JUDSON. "Cabell Stumped by Interview on Future of Northern Genius." Richmond Times-Dispatch (7 April), p. 1.
In this interview, Cabell discusses contemporary Northern writers.

6 H., W. E. Review of Ladies and Gentlemen. Boston Evening Transcript (3 November), pp. 1, 3.
For the most part, the letters in Ladies and Gentlemen are "crude saber thrusts."

7 HALBMEIER, EDWIN V. "For James Branch Cabell." The Critical Review, pp. 27-28 (The New York University Daily News Literary Supplement).
While parodying Cabell's style in Ladies and Gentlemen, the reviewer finds the book "less tender and less beautiful perhaps than the Biography, but yet provokingly and superbly erudite and witty and urbane."

8 HARTWICK, HARRY. "The Journeys of Jurgen," in his The Foreground of American Fiction. New York: American Book Company, pp. 177-186 and passim.
The author provides a study of the ways in which Cabell "itches to escape from this pedestrian world, this crass Suburbia." The author also presents an overview of Cabell's works.

9 HOWARD, LEON. "Figures of Allegory: A Study of James Branch Cabell." The Sewanee Review, 42 (1934), pp. 54-66.
The author pinpoints and analyzes the pessimism in Cabell's major comedies.

10 KINGSBURY, EDWARD M. "Branch Cabell Writes to the Dead." New York Times Book Review (7 October), p. 2.
The reviewer finds Ladies and Gentlemen to be "a good show, calculated to give pleasure--and pain."

11 LE BRETON, MAURICE. "James Branch Cabell, romancier." Revue Anglo-Américaine, 12 (February), 223-238.
Part 2 of 1933.B7.

12 MATTHEWS, T. S. Review of Smirt. The New Republic, 78 (18 April), 284.
"Mr. Cabell is a snob, and an American snob is almost a traitor to his country."

13 PRUETTE, LORINE. "Cabell Follows Alice Through the Glass." New York Herald Tribune Books (11 March), p. 5.

The reviewer is not sure what Cabell is doing in Smirt.

14 PRUETTE, LORINE. "On The Accident of Historic Reputations." New York Herald Tribune Books (7 October), p. 6.

The reviewer finds Ladies and Gentlemen to be an "inquiry into the vagaries of the human mind."

15 VAN DOREN, CARL. "Treatise on Immortals." The Nation, 139 (17 October), 449-450.

"Ladies and Gentlemen is another ironical, deft, enlivening book" for Cabell's admirers.

1935 A BOOKS--NONE

1935 B SHORTER WRITINGS

1 ANON. "Cabell 'Absent' to Felicitations." Richmond News Leader (8 April), p. 8.

Cabell is "not at home" to a newspaper reporter who seeks to interview him regarding a report that Mae West considers him one of the seven men who most appeal to her.

2 ANON. "Page Mr. Cabell! Mae West Would Like to Meet Him." Richmond Times-Dispatch (8 April), pp. 1, 8.

Cabell is listed among several prominent men Miss West is said to admire.

3 ANON. "Gone To Hollywood Cabell Declares, But Stays Home." Richmond Times-Dispatch (9 April), p. 3.

The author writes a news story in which Cabell reflects on what it would be like to know Mae West.

4 ANON. "Cabell Volume On Sale Today." Richmond News Leader (30 September), p. 6.

The author provides a news story announcing the publication of Smith.

5 ANON. "An Immortal in Letters." Arts and Decoration, 34 (November), 21, 48.

The author provides a brief introduction to Cabell and his works, finding that he is "the one living author in this country whose immortality is assured."

1935

6 BENÉT, WILLIAM ROSE. "Lord of the Forest." Saturday Review of Literature, 12 (12 October), 12.
"The hand of the author has not lost its cunning." The reader "will find both beauty and humor" in Smith.

7 BERRYMAN, JOHN McALPIN. "Types of Pedantry." The Nation, 141 (27 November), 630.
In reviewing Smith, the writer reiterates Cabell's idea that nothing lovely or worthwhile persists.

8 BULLUCK, R. D., JR. "The Cream of the Jest." Notes and Queries, 17 (August), 115.
The author provides a note on the origin of the title of the book.

9 FISHER, VARDIS. The Neurotic Nightingale. Milwaukee, Wisconsin: Casanova Press, pp. 22-38.
In a general chapter on humor, the author makes passing references to Cabell.

10 FISHER, VARDIS. We Are Betrayed. Caldwell, Idaho: Caxton Printers, 309 pp.
This novel makes literary use of Cabell.

11 GLASGOW, ELLEN. "Branch Cabell Still Clings to his Unbelief." New York Herald Tribune Books (6 October), p. 7.
"Mr. Cabell has shown yet again in 'Smith' the constancy to cling to his unbelief and the courage to place his hopeless hope in disillusionment."

12 HATCHER, HARLAN. "James Branch Cabell," in his Creating the Modern American Novel. New York: Farrar and Rinehart, pp. 191-201.
The author finds that Cabell is a romanticist writing in an age of realism.

*13 HEVESI, ANDRAS. "James Branch Cabell," in Mai Amerikai Dekameron. Edited by Jozsef Remenyi. Budapest.
Unlocatable, cited in Brewer, 1957.A1.

14 MARSH, FRED T. "Branch Cabell's 'Smith.'" New York Times Book Review (13 October), p. 6.
The reviewer provides a summary of the book, concluding that Cabell "is a rare and gifted ironist in whom we miss a certain balance."

15 MEADE, JULIAN R. I Live in Virginia. New York: Longmans, Green, pp. 190-196.

The author reports statements that Cabell is purported to have made and then reports the results of an interview with him.

16 RANSOM, JOHN CROWE. "Modern with the Southern Accent." The Virginia Quarterly Review, 11 (April), 184-200.
The author provides a general essay on Southern writing with comments about Cabell.

17 SCHRIFTGIESSER, EDWARD B. Review of Smith. Boston Evening Transcript (13 November), 3, p. 3.
Although Smith adds little to what Cabell has already said, it "continues his tradition of urbane irony."

18 SPOTSWOOD, C. M. The Unpredictable Adventure. New York: Doubleday, Doran. 456 pp.
The author makes dramatic use of Cabell and of Jurgen.

1936 A BOOKS--NONE

1936 B SHORTER WRITINGS

1 BOYNTON, PERCY H. "James Branch Cabell," in his Literature and American Life. Boston: Ginn, pp. 796-800 and passim.
The author provides an overview of Cabell's fiction, concluding that he should not be taken seriously.

2 DeCASSERES, BENJAMIN. "James Branch Cabell," in his The Elect and the Damned. New York: Privately Published, pp. 45-57.
After discussing Cabell's contribution to mythology, the author finds that he "is an original in that he has given us in his legends...the first cosmic cosmology...."

3 FISHER, VARDIS. No Villain Need Be. Caldwell, Idaho: Caxton Printers, 387 pp.
This novel makes literary use of Cabell.

4 JACK, PETER MUNRO. "The James Branch Cabell Period," in After the Genteel Tradition. Edited by Malcolm Cowley. Carbondale: Southern Illinois University Press, pp. 114-123.
The author provides an overview of the writers of the 1920s, concluding that Cabell had nothing "better to offer than the escape from it by way of Jurgen."

5 JENCKS, E. N. Review of Preface to the Past. Springfield, Massachusetts, Republican (15 February), p. 6.

The reviewer finds that Cabell's prefaces reveal his attitude toward his writing as well as his difficulties with publishers.

6 KINGSBURY, EDWARD M. "Mr. Cabell Considers His Past." New York Times Book Review (16 February), p. 2.
The reviewer wishes that Cabell would not "tinker" with his books and rewrite them.

7 KRONENBERGER, LOUIS. "Necropolis." The Nation, 142 (4 March), 286.
"Cabell as a major artist has been plainly a failure...."

8 PATERSON, ISABEL. Review of Preface to the Past. New York Herald Tribune Books (16 February), p. 4.
The reviewer takes the occasion of the publication of the book to trace Cabell's literary reception since the turn of the century.

9 QUINN, ARTHUR HOBSON. "Booth Tarkington and the Later Romance," in his American Fiction. New York: D. Appleton--Century, pp. 608-615.
The author provides an overview of Cabell's works, noting "the quick decline of his vogue," which probably was caused "from an inherent flaw, a lack of sincerity, both moral and artistic." Reprinted 1964.B5.

10 RASCOE, BURTON. "Of the Brave Exciting Days when Cabell was the Subject of a Gory Literary Dog-Fight." Esquire, 5 (April), 103, 191-194.
The author recounts his discovery of Cabell's works and discusses his rise to fame.

11 SCHRIFTGIESSER, E. B. Review of Preface to the Past. Boston Evening Transcript (29 February), p. 4.
The book gives the reader a clear understanding of Cabell's "long, strange and beautiful allegory," but it "assumes in the reader a wide acquaintance with the author's other books."

12 WHITE, LEIGH. "Mr. Cabell's Dragons." The New Republic, 87 (17 June), 184.
"Unfortunately Mr. Cabell continues to amuse himself with his 'cosmic japes.'"

*13 WOODFORD, JACK. Gentleman from Parnassus. New York: Godwin.
The author makes dramatic use of Cabell in several places in this novel. Unlocatable, cited in Hall, 1974.A1.

1937 A BOOKS

1 KLIENFELTER, WALTER. Books About Poictesme: An Essay in Imaginative Bibliography. Chicago: Black Cat Press, 28 pp.
The author provides an imaginary explication of Poictesme and its inhabitants.

1937 B SHORTER WRITINGS

1 ANON. "Cabell Election Gives City 4 in Arts, Letters Institute." Richmond News Leader (21 January), pp. 1, 25.
The author provides a news story on Cabell's election to the body, along with comments about other Richmonders who are members.

2 ANON. "Monticello Club Razed in Blaze." Richmond News Leader (26 March), p. 1.
The author provides a news report on the fire that destroyed Dumbarton Grange, Cabell's former home.

3 ANON. "Cabell's Former Home Burns." Richmond Times-Dispatch (27 March), pp. 1, 3.
The author provides a news report on the fire that destroyed Dumbarton Grange, Cabell's former home. Comments by Cabell are included.

4 ANON. Review of Smire. Reading and Collecting (1 May), p. 14.
Writing in an ironic tone, the reviewer finds the novel "anti-social, un-modern and un-American."

*5 CASH, W. J. "Poictesme for the Pious." Charlotte News (20 June).
Unlocatable, cited in Brewer, 1957.A1.

6 CLEATON, IRENE and ALLEN CLEATON. "James Branch Cabell," in their Books and Battles. Boston: Houghton, Mifflin, pp. 17-22, 239-242 and passim.
The authors provide biographical notes on Cabell along with a general discussion of his works and his fictional dramatization of sex.

7 HACKETT, FRANCIS. "Pardon Me!" The New Republic, 90 (24 March), 207-208.
The author provides a discussion of Cabell and other writers of the 1920s.

1937

8 JACK, PETER MUNRO. "The James Branch Cabell Period." The New Republic, 89 (13 January), 323-326.
In a detailed discussion of the 1920s and its attitudes toward Cabell's writing, the author concludes that "Mr. Cabell has carried [the] novel of escape, pretense and sophisticated grandeur to the point of exhaustion, to the point at which it becomes a composed philosophy of life." (Reprinted in Malcolm Cowley, ed. After the Genteel Tradition. Carbondale: Southern Illinois University Press, pp. 114-123.)

9 LOGGINS, VERNON. "Cap and Bells," in his I Hear America. New York: Thomas Y. Crowell, pp. 287-296.
The author provides an introductory appraisal of Cabell and his works, finding him a realist rather than a romanticist.

10 McCOLE, C. JOHN. "Branch Cabell," in his Lucifer at Large. London: Longmans, Green, pp. 57-81.
Although, the author notes, "Cabell can be dull..., he is a writer who looks at the world with the eyes of disillusion.... So it is that Cabell escapes to Poictesme...."

11 MARSH, FRED T. "Branch Cabell Closes a Trilogy." New York Times Book Review (28 March), p. 2.
The reviewer finds that "the urbanity runs a little thin at times. The irony is a little shrill"; but, he concludes, "let us have more of this fantasy."

12 MULLER, HERBERT J. Review of Smire. Saturday Review of Literature, 15 (10 April), 12.
The reviewer finds the book to be "less adequate, moving, and interesting" than those of the major writers.

13 PRUETTE, LORINE. "Suave, Mocking and Pitiful." New York Herald Tribune Books (11 April), p. 6.
In reviewing Smire, the reviewer complains that Cabell is not concerned with the present world.

14 RASCOE, BURTON. "The Hughes-Cabell Scrap," in his Before I Forget. New York: The Literary Guild, pp. 386-395.
Introduced by an editorial statement, the letters between Rupert Hughes and Cabell, regarding the former's objection to Beyond Life being serialized in the Chicago Tribune, are reproduced.

15 SMITH, CAROLINE. Review of Smire. The Nation, 144 (3 April), 389.

The reviewer admits that she does not understand the book.

16 WESTEN, HERBERT. "Mr. Cabell Regards the Inevitable." Richmond Times-Dispatch Sunday Magazine (21 March), pp. 3, 12.
The author reports on an interview with Cabell.

1938 A BOOKS--NONE

1938 B SHORTER WRITINGS

1 AYER, THOMAS P. "Branch Cabell at Best in New York." Richmond Times-Dispatch Sunday Magazine (30 October), p. 12.
In a review of The King Was in His Counting House, the writer concludes that "All who chuckled with Jurgen will do so again over Mr. Cabell's latest work."

2 CHUBB, THOMAS CALDECOT. "Mr. Cabell Returns Near to Poictesme." New York Times Book Review (9 October), p. 2.
While reviewing The King Was in His Counting House, the writer finds that he has grown tired of Cabell, but that the book has merit as a moral tale.

3 DAVENPORT, BASIL. "Not Magic, After All." Saturday Review of Literature, 18 (22 October), 11-12.
The reviewer describes the contents of The King Was in His Counting House and then complains that "the old flavor is gone" from Cabell's writings.

4 FISHER, VARDIS. Forgive Us Our Virtues: A Comedy of Evasions. Caldwell, Idaho: Caxton Printers, 447 pp.
The novel makes dramatic use of Cabell.

5 HOWARD, JOHN MELVILLE. "The Fate of Mr. Cabell." Reading and Collecting, 2 (January), 5-7.
The author provides a general appraisal of Cabell as a writer whose popularity has waned and whose books have descended in importance for collectors. He speculates that the prices will rise, however, and includes a list of Cabellian collectibles.

6 PRUETTE, LORINE. "Cabell's Fair Ladies." New York Herald Tribune Books (16 October), p. 7.
In a review of The King Was in His Counting House, the reviewer finds the theme of the book to be altruism.

1938

7 SEHRT, ERNST THEODOR. "Die Weltanschauung James Branch Cabells (im Anschluss an seinen Roman Figures of Earth)." Englische Studien, 72 (August), 355-399.
The author provides a general appraisal of Cabell's philosophy as expressed in his novels.

8 TINKER, EDWARD LAROCQUE. "New Editions." New York Times Book Review (22 May), p. 21.
The reviewer speculates that Of Ellen Glasgow will become "a rare and sought for collector's item."

1940 A BOOKS--NONE

1940 B SHORTER WRITINGS

1 BOYNTON, PERCY H. "James Branch Cabell," in his America in Contemporary Fiction. Chicago: University of Chicago Press, pp. 73-90.
Reprint of 1924.B9.

2 DAVENPORT, BASIL. "In the Lineage of 'Jurgen.'" Saturday Review of Literature, 31 (27 January), 11.
In reviewing Hamlet Had an Uncle, the writer finds that the book is as good as Jurgen, "but no one will call it a masterpiece."

3 ESHELMAN, LLOYD. "Mr. Cabell Presents His Hamlet." New York Times Book Review (28 January), p. 7.
The reviewer recommends Hamlet Had an Uncle as an antidote to thinking about war.

4 FREEMAN, DOUGLAS SOUTHALL. Review of Hamlet Had an Uncle. Richmond News Leader (29 January), p. 10.
The reviewer finds that the novel "deals brilliantly with one of the most renowned and certainly the most distorted theme in literature." The book "will be one of the most widely read of Mr. Cabell's works since Jurgen."

5 MAIR, JOHN. Review of Hamlet Had an Uncle. The New Statesman and Nation, 20 (14 September), 268-269.
The reviewer finds that Cabell, "in short, has provided a memorable specimen of small-town sophistication, and reminded his many admirers that you can't judge the novel by the name upon the jacket."

6 MILLETT, FRED B. "James Branch Cabell," in his Contemporary American Authors. New York: Harcourt, Brace, pp. 276-280.
The author provides a biographical sketch of Cabell, followed by a primary and secondary checklist on him.

7 O'BRIEN, KATE. Review of Hamlet Had an Uncle. The Spectator (30 August), pp. 226-228.
The novel "is an amusing and urbane piece of foolery. But the farce does, I think, drag on too long, and the central joke is a little too obvious...."

8 RASCOE, BURTON. "Mencken, Nathan, and Cabell." The American Mercury, 49 (March), 366.
"In this prose comedy--[Hamlet Had an Uncle]--Cabell is at his pristine best...."

9 TAYLOR, DEEMS. The Well Tempered Listener. New York: Simon and Schuster, p. 239.
The author finds that the music critics were in error when they wrote about his musical adaptation of Jurgen.

10 VAN DOREN, CARL. "James Branch Cabell," in his The American Novel, 1789-1939. New York: Macmillan, pp. 315-322.
The author views Cabell and his works in retrospect, concluding that Jurgen, The Cream of the Jest, and The High Place "promise to outlive" all his other works.

11 Works Progress Administration Writers Program. Virginia. New York: Oxford, pp. 162-163, 166, 288, 297.
Passing references to Cabell and his works.

1941 A BOOKS--NONE

1941 B SHORTER WRITINGS

1 CARGILL, OSCAR. Intellectual America. New York: Macmillan, pp. 495-497.
The author finds that Cabell "is, beyond all doubt, the most tedious person who has achieved high repute as a literatus in America...." In addition, Cargill continues, Cabell's "reputation as a stylist is overblown." Finally, he is no more than a descendant of the "minor British and American romantics of the late nineteenth century...."

1942

1942 A BOOKS--NONE

1942 B SHORTER WRITINGS

1 ANON. Review of The First Gentleman of America. The New Yorker, 17 (7 February), 61-62.
"Although his story is, for a change, set in a real country and has some basis in historical fact, Mr. Cabell's style of narration has not changed."

2 ANON. "Cabell the Historian." Richmond News Leader (23 April), p. 10.
The writer notes that, contrary to what reviewers are saying, The First Gentleman of America is grounded in fact.

3 BREWSTER, PAUL G. "Jurgen and Figures of Earth and the Russian Skazki." American Literature, 13 (January), 305-319.
The author explores Cabell's indebtedness to Russian tales.

4 BULLOCK, FLORENCE HAXTON. "Demi-Godson of the Lord." New York Herald Tribune Books (25 January), p. 7.
The First Gentleman of America is, "All in all, delightful."

5 DIXON, ROBERT. "Cabell Turns Back Years as Old Police Court Closes." Richmond News Leader (30 April), p. 3.
The author provides a news story recounting Cabell's visit to the court in which he was once a police reporter.

6 DUTCHER, HOWARD. "Cabell's Book Spicy Volume of 1500s." Richmond News Leader (31 January), p. 5.
The First Gentleman of America is urbane, naughty and witty. Further, "tremendous research went into the making of the book."

7 HUNTER, THOMAS LOMAX. "As it Appears to the Cavalier." Richmond Times-Dispatch (28 January), p. 10.
The author tells the plot of The First Gentleman of America and then recommends the book.

8 JOHNSON, MERLE. Merle Johnson's American First Editions. Edited by Jacob Blanck. New York: R. R. Bowker, pp. 87-91.
The compiler lists Cabell's first editions and provides a partial listing of his contributions to magazines. Revised and reprinted 1965.B7.

9 KAZIN, ALFRED. On Native Grounds. New York: Harcourt, 541 pp., passim.
The author makes several references to Cabell.

10 KUNITZ, STANLEY J. and HARRISON HAYCRAFT. "James Branch Cabell," in their Twentieth Century Authors. New York: Wilson, 1577 pp.
The authors provide a brief biographical sketch.

11 MARSH, FRED T. "Mr. Cabell's Comedy." New York Times Book Review (1 February), p. 6.
The reviewer finds The First Gentleman of America to be one of Cabell's best books. He especially likes "its origin, theme and setting."

12 RASCOE, BURTON. "The First Writing Gentleman of Virginia." Chicago Sun (14 February), p. 16.
The author provides a reappraisal of Cabell's writing career.

13 REDMAN, BEN RAY. Review of The First Gentleman of America. Saturday Review of Literature, 25 (7 February), 7.
The reviewer comments on Cabell's style and use of irony in the book. He also notes that Cabell's books are now out of vogue.

14 Who's Who in America. Chicago: A. N. Marquis, p. 453.
This edition of Who's Who contains a biographical entry on Cabell.

1943 A BOOKS--NONE

1943 B SHORTER WRITINGS

*1 DERLETH, AUGUST. "The St. Johns Added to Rivers Series." Chicago Sun Book Week (5 September).
Unlocatable, cited in Brewer, 1957.A1.

2 FIRESTONE, CLARK B. Review of The St. Johns. Saturday Review of Literature (11 September), p. 7.
The reviewer finds the book "scintillating, cynical, and singularly candid."

3 KENNEDY, STETSON. Review of The St. Johns. New York Times Book Review (5 September), p. 7.

The reviewer finds that the book is better than either Cabell or A. J. Hanna could have produced alone. It "sets a high-water mark among the two dozen great river books which have preceded it."

4 RAWLINGS, MARJORIE KINNAN. "A River that Flows Through Florida History." New York Herald Tribune Book Review (5 September), p. 3.
The reviewer finds the modern characters dull, but the book "transcends any immediate mediocrity."

1946 A BOOKS--NONE

1946 B SHORTER WRITINGS

1 ANON. Review of There Were Two Pirates. Kirkus, 4 (1 June), 259.
"This isn't straight Cabell...; this is fantasy, but not erotica...done with effortless veiled humor."

2 ANON. "Mr. Cabell's Mammy." Richmond Times-Dispatch (9 June), 4, p. 1.
This article centers on Cabell's mention of his nurse Mrs. Louisa Nelson.

3 ANON. Review of There Were Two Pirates. New Yorker, 22 (17 August), 88.
The reviewer finds the book to be "the best summer reading of the year."

4 ANON. "Ghost from the Past." Time, 48 (19 August), 102.
"Most readers will find Two Pirates as transparent and embarrassing as any other ghost from the past."

5 ANON. "Pro & Con Cabell." Richmond Times-Dispatch (23 August), p. 14.
The author notes upon the publication of There Were Two Pirates that the reviewers are still divided regarding Cabell.

6 ANON. Review of There Were Two Pirates. Current History, 11 (December), 512.
"The only fault is in its brevity."

7 CULVER, JOHN W. "James Branch Cabell." Andean Quarterly (Winter), pp. 32-37.
The author provides an overview of Cabell and his works.

8 GORDON, ARMISTEAD C., JR. "Mellow, Triune Cabell." New York Times Book Review (11 August), p. 5.
"Entertaining as it is, There Were Two Pirates...remains considerably this side of greatness...."

9 GUILFOIL, KENSLEY. "Cabell Retains Old Power." Chicago Sunday Tribune Magazine of Books (11 August), p. 3.
There Were Two Pirates is "one of the most exquisite specimens of prose of recent years."

10 HART, H. W. Review of There Were Two Pirates. Library Journal, 71 (August), 1049.
The reviewer finds the book to be a "graceful variation on a theme from legend, but a slight addition to the Cabell shelf."

11 HUTCHENS, JOHN K. "East Coast, West Coast--and Mr. Cabell." New York Times Book Review (1 September), p. 10.
The author recounts the plagiarism charge brought by E. D. Lambright against Cabell. Reprinted in the Richmond Times-Dispatch (5 September), p. 8.

12 PRESCOTT, ORVILLE. Review of There Were Two Pirates. Yale Review, 36 (September), 189-192.
The reviewer finds the book to be "exactly of the same variety as Mr. Cabell has been producing for forty years. And that variety has long since worn threadbare."

13 REDMAN, BEN RAY. Review of There Were Two Pirates. Saturday Review of Literature, 29 (10 August), 7-8.
While commenting on the contents of the book, the reviewer notes that it is typical of Cabell's many well done volumes.

14 SUGRUE, THOMAS. Review of There Were Two Pirates. New York Herald Tribune Weekly Book Review (11 August), p. 3.
The reviewer compares the book's main character to Cabell's Dom Manuel. He finds that ultimately the story becomes monotonous.

1947 A BOOKS--NONE

1947 B SHORTER WRITINGS

1 ANON. Review of There Were Two Pirates. Theatre Arts, 31 (January), 71.
The reviewer finds the book to be a "charming fable."

1947

2 BUTCHER, FANNY. "The Literary Spotlight." Chicago Sunday Tribune Books (20 April), p. 10.
The author reminisces about Cabell, noting his decline in popularity.

3 KUNSTLER, WILLIAM M. Review of Let Me Lie. Atlantic Monthly, 179 (May), 160.
The reviewer praises Cabell's "charm" and "detached exuberance."

4 MATTHEWS, ALLEN R. "Off the Bookshelves." Richmond Times-Dispatch (9 March), 4, p. 7.
In commenting upon the forthcoming Let Me Lie, the author finds that Cabell, "frequently an acid writer, cannot dodge the fact that he is also a becomingly modest writer."

5 MOSELEY, D. H. Review of Let Me Lie. Commonweal, 46 (18 April), 22.
The reviewer finds the book to be "old" as well as "a tiresome swan song."

6 NORTON, DAN S. Review of Let Me Lie. New York Times Book Review (30 March), p. 5.
The book "is a collection of stylistic devices designed to conceal the fact that the author has nothing in particular to say. It is an elegy for the elegist."

7 RASCOE, BURTON. "Cabell Analyzes Certain Virginia Myths." New York Herald Tribune Books (30 March), p. 7.
The reviewer finds the book to be a good antidote to the "bilious" literary fare of the day.

8 WILSON, JAMES SOUTHALL. "Cabellian Tribute to Virginia." The Virginia Quarterly Review, 23 (Summer), 452-455.
The reviewer comments on what it means to be a Virginian and then compares Let Me Lie to his findings.

9 WITHAM, W. TASKER. "James Branch Cabell," in his Panorama of American Literature. New York: Stephen Day, pp. 257-259.
The author finds that Cabell is an opponent of modern day realism.

1948 A BOOKS--NONE

1948 B SHORTER WRITINGS

1 ALLEN, MORSE. Review of The Witch-Woman. Hartford Courant (4 July), p. 14.

"Baffled by philosophy," the reviewer finds, Cabell "has found relief in the melody of prose rhythm."

2 BARNETT, DAVID L. "Cabell Finishes Fiftieth Book--Possibly Last." Richmond News Leader (30 October), p. 3.

The writer conducts a brief interview with Cabell upon the occasion of the publication of The Devil's Own Dear Son.

3 BUTCHER, FANNY. "The Literary Spotlight." Chicago Sunday Tribune Magazine of Books (9 May), 4, p. 2.

The author provides brief comments on Cabell and his homelife, noting that his writing is no longer "in vogue."

4 HAWKINS, NINA. "James Branch Cabell's Publishers Planning for Reprints of Earlier Works." St. Augustine Record (14 April), p. 2.

The writer notes that a series of Cabell's reprints is underway and also comments on Cabell's yearly trips to Florida and on other biographical items.

5 HIMELICK, RAYMOND. "Cabell, Shelley and the 'Incorrigible Flesh.'" South Atlantic Quarterly, 47 (January), 88-95.

The author discusses Shelley and Cabell in light of their "intense preoccupation with man's hopeful and determined quest for beauty and harmony of existence that is somehow epitomized by the woman dream." Reprinted 1974.A2.

6 MILLER, MAX. "Cabell Stirs Memories of Sophisticated '20s." San Diego Union (23 May), p. 11.

The reviewer finds that some of The Witch-Woman is new, some a rehash, but it is "Cabell all over again, whether or not we any longer sit up till after midnight quoting from him."

7 VAN VECHTEN, CARL. "Mr. Cabell of Lichfield and Poictesme." The Yale University Library Gazette, 23 (July), 1-7.

The author reminisces about his relationship with Cabell. Reprinted 1955.B8.

8 WAGENKNECHT, EDWARD. "Cabell: A Reconsideration." College English, 9 (February), 238-246.

The writer provides a reappraisal of the entire Cabell canon, concluding that "though there may be much, first and

1948

last, for which we have to forgive James Branch Cabell, he is still a unique and incomparable figure in American literature." Revised and reprinted 1952.B9.

9 WAGENKNECHT, EDWARD. Review of The Witch-Woman. Chicago Sunday Tribune Magazine of Books (23 May), 4, p. 12.
"Within these pages is to be found some of the loveliest writing that has been done in our time."

*10 WOODFORD, JACK. Traded Lives. New York.
This novel makes dramatic use of Cabell. Unlocatable, cited in Hall, 1974.A1.

1949 A BOOKS--NONE

1949 B SHORTER WRITINGS

1 ANON. Review of The Devil's Own Dear Son. New Yorker, 25 (7 May), 109.
"Altogether, a featherweight but charming novel...."

2 BOND, NELSON. The Thirty-First of February. New York: Gnome Press, 272 pp.
In the "Author's Note" Bond gives credit to Cabell, from whom he took the title for this collection of short stories.

3 CRANE, MILTON. "Restoration in St. Augustine." Saturday Review of Literature, 32 (23 April), 12.
The reviewer finds that Cabell's "old fire flickers fitfully" in The Devil's Own Dear Son, but he wishes it were something new.

4 GUERARD, ALBERT, JR. "The New Fashion." New York Times Book Review (17 April), p. 17.
By "detaching himself from all currently fashionable modes of fiction in The Devil's Own Dear Son, Mr. Cabell has honored his craft."

5 JENKINS, JIM, JR. "James Branch Cabell, at 70, Produces 50th Book." Richmond Times-Dispatch (10 April), 4, p. 1.
The author provides an interview with Cabell upon the publication of The Devil's Own Dear Son.

6 RASCOE, BURTON. "Cabell Unorthodox as Always." New York Herald Tribune Books (17 April), p. 4.
The reviewer, writing of The Devil's Own Dear Son, finds it a "miracle" that Cabell "hasn't been lynched."

7 ROBINSON, DUNCAN. "The Devil's Best Gift is a Heating System." Dallas Daily Times Herald (17 April), 7, p. 5.
"The vitality of the book, as indeed of all of Mr. Caball's works, is the style."

8 ROCKWELL, KENNETH. "A Gentleman of Virginia Celebrates His Birthday." Dallas Daily Times Herald (17 April), 7, pp. 4-5.
The author provides a general article on Cabell and his works on the occasion of his seventieth birthday.

1950 A BOOKS--NONE

1950 B SHORTER WRITINGS

1 ANON. "Cabelliana Exhibited at Yale." Richmond Times-Dispatch (26 March), 4, p. 6.
The writer provides a news story on the exhibit.

2 ANON. "James Branch Cabell Weds Ex-Richmonder." Richmond News Leader (16 June), p. 1.
The writer provides a news story on the occasion of Cabell's marriage to Margaret Waller Freeman.

3 FISHWICK, MARSHALL W. "James Branch Cabell, Virginia Novelist." Commonwealth, 17 (May), 17, 35-36.
The author provides a general introduction to and appraisal of Cabell and his works.

4 HART, JAMES D. The Popular Book. Berkeley: University of California Press, passim.
The author notes in passing the former popularity of Cabell.

5 KEMLER, EDGAR. "The Battle of the Books," in his The Irreverent Mr. Mencken. Boston: Little, Brown, passim.
There are sixteen references to Cabell in this book.

*6 MARTINALE, G. D. "Cabell as a Fantasiaste." Fantasy Advertiser (January).
Unlocatable, cited in Brewer, 1957.A1.

7 SMITH, H. ALLEN. People Named Smith. New York: Doubleday, pp. 189-190.
The writer provides a brief summary of Cabell's Smith.

1950

8 VALENTINE, ROSS. "Birthday of a Superb Artist." Richmond Times-Dispatch (14 April), p. 14.

The author provides a general article on Cabell upon the occasion of his seventieth birthday. Although the author does "not fully appreciate Mr. Cabell's writings," he finds him "an aesthete in the most commendable meaning of that word."

1951 A BOOKS--NONE

1951 B SHORTER WRITINGS

1 ANON. "Richmond Authors Will Have 'Day' on Wednesday." Richmond Times-Dispatch Sunday Magazine (13 May), p. 9.

The author provides a news story in which Cabell, and forty-one other Richmond writers, are noted as having accepted invitations to the first Richmond's Author Day.

2 HERGESHEIMER, JOSEPH. "Happy Birthday, Dear Mr. Cabell." Town and Country (April), pp. 100, 104.

The author provides impressions and reminiscences centering on his thirty year friendship with Cabell.

3 HOFFMAN, FREDERICK J. The Modern Novel in America. Chicago: Henry Regnery, pp. 116-120 and passim.

The author notes that Cabell overwrites and is needlessly obscure. "To the almost endless succession of 'romances'... Cabell brought all of his empty cultivation of style and his haphazard erudition."

4 MANCHESTER, WILLIAM. Disturber of the Peace. New York: Harper, passim.

There are sixteen scattered references to Cabell in this book.

5 MIZENER, ARTHUR. The Far Side of Paradise. New York: Houghton, Mifflin, 362 pp.

This book contains comments about Burton Rascoe's charge that F. Scott Fitzgerald imitated Cabell.

6 QUINN, ARTHUR HOBSON. The Literature of the American People. New York: Appleton-Century-Crofts, p. 889.

The author provides a two-paragraph appraisal of Cabell, calling him by "all odds the most persistent unreconstructed romanticist in contemporary letters."

7 WARFEL, HARRY R. "James Branch Cabell," in his American Novelists of Today. New York: American Book Co., pp. 71-74.
The author provides a general appraisal of Cabell and his works.

1952 A BOOKS--NONE

1952 B SHORTER WRITINGS

1 ANON. "Books." New Yorker, 28 (23 February), 106.
"All in all," Quiet Please is "a very civilized and amusing little caper."

2 ANON. "Books." Time, 69 (25 February), 48.
The reviewer notes that Cabell's Quiet Please indicates that Cabell has spent "a lifelong career blowing literary soap bubbles and is now sinking into an amiable senescence."

3 ANON. "Cabell's Novel Publication Set Later in Year." Richmond News Leader (28 March), p. 6.
The author provides a news account of the forthcoming publication of Cabell's fifty-first book along with comments on the unveiling of the sculptured head of Cabell done by sculptor Hollis W. Holbrook.

4 BROOKS, VAN WYCK. The Confident Years. New York: E. P. Dutton, pp. 342-347 and passim.
The author provides a general appraisal of Cabell's works before World War One, concentrating on his medievalism.

5 KRUTCH, JOSEPH WOOD. Review of Quiet Please. The Nation, 174 (23 February), 180.
The reviewer notes that Cabell will never be able to say what he wants to say and still be widely accepted.

6 LYELL, FRANK H. "The Hedonistic Mr. Cabell." New York Times Book Review (23 March), p. 20.
While reviewing Quiet Please the author notes that Cabell is no longer read. He also comments on Cabell's affected style in the present book.

7 PARKS, EDD WINFIELD. "James Branch Cabell." Hopkins Review, 5 (Summer), 37-47.
The author provides an overall appraisal of Cabell's literary career.

1952

8 SCHERMAN, DAVID E. and ROSEMARIE REDLICH. "James Branch Cabell," in their Literary America. New York: Dodd, Mead, pp. 140-141.
Writing about The First Gentleman of America, the authors conclude that "Cabell was the supreme escapist of his day."

9 WAGENKNECHT, EDWARD. "James Branch Cabell," in his Cavalcade of the American Novel. New York: Holt, pp. 339-352.
Revised and reprinted 1948.B8.

1953 A BOOKS--NONE

1953 B SHORTER WRITINGS

1 FISHER, VARDIS. God or Caesar? Caldwell, Idaho: Caxton Printers, passim.
This book contains nineteen references to various aspects of Cabell's works.

2 PARKS, EDD WINFIELD. "James Branch Cabell," in Southern Renascence. Edited by Louis D. Rubin, Jr. and Robert Jacobs. Baltimore: Johns Hopkins, pp. 251-261.
The author provides an essay that views Cabell in light of twentieth century literature in the South.

1954 A BOOKS--NONE

1954 B SHORTER WRITINGS

1 GLASGOW, ELLEN. The Woman Within. New York: Harcourt, Brace.
In chapter eleven of this posthumously published autobiography, the author reminisces about Cabell and the murder and homosexual scandals in which he was allegedly involved as a young man.

2 HUBBELL, JAY B. The South in American Literature, 1607-1900. Durham, North Carolina: Duke University Press, pp. 845-846.
The author provides general comments on Cabell's works, concluding that "whatever the setting, his works could hardly have been written outside of the South."

3 STARR, NATHAN C. King Arthur Today: The Arthurian Legend in English and American Literature, 1901-1953. Gainesville: University of Florida Press, pp. 113-114.

The author provides a discussion of Jurgen as derivative of the Arthurian legend.

1955 A BOOKS--NONE

1955 B SHORTER WRITINGS

1 CAMPBELL, HARRY MODEAN. "Notes on Religion in the Southern Renascence." Shenandoah, 6 (Summer), 10-18.
Cabell is an extreme case. He "ironically denies the existence of his dream world...at the very moment of proclaiming its ideal beauty." He yearns to recover beliefs ever lost.

2 FRIDDELL, GUY. "Book Called Autobiography but Local Author Says it Isn't." Richmond News Leader (31 October), p. 21.
The author provides an interview with Cabell upon the publication of As I Remember It.

3 LEWIS, GRACE HEGGER [Mrs. Telesforo Casanova]. With Love From Gracie. New York: Harcourt, Brace, passim.
This book contains a number of references to the Cabell-Sinclair Lewis friendship.

4 POPE, BEN. "Richmond Authors Cabell, Dowdey Express Views on Literature of Today." Richmond Times-Dispatch (4 December), E, p. 2.
The author provides an interview with the two writers.

5 RASCOE, BURTON. Review of As I Remember It. Chicago Sunday Tribune (20 November), p. 2.
This is "by long odds the tenderest, the most touching, the most compassionate, and, in some ways, the most revealing of his many books." Especially important are the character studies of Ellen Glasgow, John Macy, Guy Holt, and Hugh Walpole.

6 SCHROETTER, HILDA NOEL. "Getting to Know Mr. Cabell." Richmond Times-Dispatch (6 November), F, p. 5.
The reviewer finds that "seldom has a writer consciously revealed so much of himself as Mr. Cabell does" in As I Remember It.

7 SMITH, ELLEN HART. "James Branch Cabell: Two Books In One." New York Herald Tribune Books (6 November), p. 12.
The reviewer discusses Priscilla Bradley Cabell and her relationship to As I Remember It.

1955

8 VAN VECHTEN, CARL. Fragments from an Unwritten Autobiography. New Haven: Yale University Press, Volume 1, pp. 21-35.
Reprint of 1948.B7.

9 WALBRIDGE, E. F. Review of As I Remember It. Library Journal, 80 (1 December), 2775.
The remainder of the book does not measure up to the first part, but the reviewer recommends it for library purchase.

1956 A BOOKS--NONE

1956 B SHORTER WRITINGS

1 BERTI, LUIGI. "Lo strano caso di James Branch Cabell." Inventairo, 8 (1956), 248-266.
The author provides a retrospective article, in which he discusses Cabell's style, world view, and the causes for his decline in popularity.

2 BOWLES, MARTHA MARY HOADLY. "I Played Scrabble with James Branch Cabell." The Leaguer, 29 (March), 5.
The author provides brief notes on the reading of James Joyce's Ulysses with side comments about Cabell.

3 HIMELICK, RAYMOND. "Figures of Cabell." Modern Fiction Studies, 2 (Winter 1956-57), 214-220.
The author provides a critical article that examines Cabell's world view. Reprinted 1974.A2.

4 PARKS, EDD WINFIELD. "Cabell's Cream of the Jest." Modern Fiction Studies, 2 (May), 68-70.
The reviewer discusses Cabell's use of the phrase "the cream of the jest," finding that to him the jest is that man lives only by his dreams.

5 RUBIN, LOUIS D., JR. "The Prospects of a Cabell Revival." Richmond News Leader (5 June), p. 10.
In this editorial, the writer suggests the possibility that a Cabell revival is on the way.

6 RUBIN, LOUIS D., JR. "James Branch Cabell Today." Baltimore Evening Sun (6 July), p. 20.
The author provides an interview with Cabell.

7 WILSON, EDMUND. "The James Branch Cabell Case Reopened." New Yorker, 32 (21 April), 140-168.
In this extended and penetrating article, occasioned by the publication of As I Remember It, the author concludes that Cabell is better than he had remembered him as being. Reprinted in his The Bit Between My Teeth. New York: Farrar and Straus, pp. 291-325.

8 ZOLLA, ELÉMIRE. "Il Jurgen di Joseph [sic] Branch Cabell." Studi Americani, 2 (1956), 195-205.
In a critical article on Jurgen, the author places the book in the context of American literature of the 1920s.

1957 A BOOKS

1 BREWER, FRANCES JOAN. James Branch Cabell: A Bibliography of His Writings, Biography and Criticism. Charlottesville: University Press of Virginia, 206 pp.
The compiler provides collations and notations on Cabell's books, along with his contributions to other books and periodicals. Included also is secondary criticism in books, pamphlets, and periodicals. Cabell wrote the preface for the book. Reprinted 1971.A1.

2 BRUCCOLI, MATTHEW J. James Branch Cabell: A Bibliography, Part II: Notes on the Cabell Collections at the University of Virginia. Charlottesville: University Press of Virginia, 178 pp.
"This work is basically a listing of all the impressions of all the editions of James Branch Cabell's works now in the Alderman Library of the University of Virginia.... Whenever the material was available, Mr. Cabell's books have been exposed to a sample collation" on the Hinman Collating Machine.

1957 B SHORTER WRITINGS

1 FISHWICK, MARSHALL. "Cabell and Glasgow: Tradition in Search of Meaning." Shenandoah, 8 (Summer), 24-35.
The author provides a general assessment of Cabell's works, noting that he "satirizes his own aristocratic heritage, and the tastes and habits of Virginia."

1958 A BOOKS--NONE

1958

1958 B SHORTER WRITINGS

1 ANON. "Cabell Rites to Be Here Tomorrow." Richmond News Leader (6 May), pp. 1, 3.
Obituary.

2 ANON. "James Branch Cabell, 79, Succumbs Here." Richmond Times-Dispatch (6 May), pp. 1, 7.
Obituary.

3 COWAN, LOUISE. "The End of the Fugitive," in her The Fugitive Group. Baton Rouge: Louisiana State University Press, p. 215.
In a short note, the author finds that Allen Tate's poem "To a Romantic Novelist" in the September 1925 issue of The Fugitive is directed against Cabell.

4 FISHWICK, MARSHALL. "Two Roads from Eden." Modern Age, 2 (Fall), 404-407.
In a general assessment of Cabell's works, the author finds that like Ellen Glasgow he did not escape his Southern environment.

5 MacDONALD, EDGAR E. "Cabell Without Jurgen." Randolph-Macon College Bulletin, 29 (September), 7-8, 26-27.
The author recounts Cabell's contribution to literature, along with his attitudes toward the South, calling for "a reassessment of his place in our literary history."

6 PARRINGTON, VERNON. "James Branch Cabell," in his Main Currents in American Thought. Volume 3. New York: Harcourt, Brace, pp. 335-345.
Reprint of 1921.B41.

7 TARRANT, DESMOND. "James Branch Cabell: A Reappraisal." British Association for American Studies Bulletin, No. 7, pp. 37-45.
The author provides a general discussion of Cabell as a mythmaker. Reprinted in Shenandoah, 9 (Summer), 3-9.

8 WILSON, EDMUND. "James Branch Cabell: 1879-1958." The Nation, 186 (7 June), 519-520.
The author provides an obituary tribute and assessment of Cabell's place in literature. "His steadfastness and self-respect will be more conspicuous to the future...than it has recently been to us." Reprinted 1965.B8.

1959 A BOOKS--NONE

1959 B SHORTER WRITINGS

1 HIMELICK, RAYMOND. "Cabell and the Modern Temper." The South Atlantic Quarterly, 58 (Spring), 176-184.
In this general critical article, the author finds that "Cabell's most interesting work has been a parable, an abstract of life's...triviality." Reprinted 1974.A2.

2 RUBIN, LOUIS D., JR. No Place on Earth: Ellen Glasgow, James Branch Cabell and Richmond-in-Virginia. Austin: University of Texas Press, 81 pp.
A substantial portion of this volume is given to a discussion of Cabell.

3 SCHLEGEL, DOROTHY. "James Branch Cabell and Southern Romanticism," in The South in Perspective. Edited by Francis Butler Simkins. Farmville, Virginia: Longwood College, pp. 31-48.
The author argues that it was Southern Romanticism that provided Cabell with "the initial dynamics governing his philosophy of life and art." Reprinted 1964.B6.

1960 A BOOKS--NONE

1960 B SHORTER WRITINGS

1 THORP, WILLARD. American Writing in the Twentieth Century. Cambridge, Massachusetts: Harvard University Press, pp. 53-54 and passim.
In a brief discussion of Jurgen, the author notes that Cabell was the novelist "who best represents the liberated spirit" of the early 1920s.

1961 A BOOKS--NONE

1961 B SHORTER WRITINGS

1 BOOTH, WAYNE. The Rhetoric of Fiction. Chicago: University of Chicago Press, pp. 288-289.
In a brief discussion of Cabell's works, the author notes that "Much of James Branch Cabell...is designed to break

down the reader's conventional notions of what is real, and an essential part of this polemic is the attempt to undermine the reader's normal trust in what the narrator says."

2 MENCKEN, H. L. Letters of H. L. Mencken. Edited by Guy J. Forgue. New York: Alfred A. Knopf, passim.
References to Cabell appear on twenty separate pages.

3 RUBIN, LOUIS D., JR. "Two in Richmond: Ellen Glasgow and James Branch Cabell," in his and Robert D. Jacobs' South: Modern Literature In Its Cultural Setting. Garden City, New York: Doubleday, pp. 115-141.
The author provides a discussion of Cabell and his peers against the backdrop of the Richmond, and Southern, cultural and historical milieu. Reprinted 1967.B19.

4 SCHLEGEL, DOROTHY B. "Cabell and His Critics," in The Dilemma of the Southern Writer. Edited by Richard K. Meeker. Farmville, Virginia: Institute of Southern Culture Studies, pp. 119-140.
The author explores Cabell's relationship to his critics, noting that he "felt that it was next to impossible" to please them, "especially his Southern critics." Reprinted 1971.B10.

5 SCHORER, MARK. Sinclair Lewis: An American Life. New York: McGraw Hill, 867 pp.
Because Lewis and Cabell were once close friends, this book contains numerous references to the latter.

6 SILVETTE, HERBERT ["BARNABY DOGBOLT"]. Never Say Die. London: Christopher Johnson, 233 pp.
This novel makes literary use of Cabell, who appears as the character Campbell Twigg.

1962 A BOOKS

1 COLUM, PADRAIC and MARGARET FREEMAN CABELL. Between Friends: Letters of James Branch Cabell and Others. New York: Harcourt, Brace and World, 304 pp.
The editors reproduce selected letters of Cabell and his literary acquaintances, centering primarily on the suppression and trial of Jurgen.

2 DAVIS, JOE LEE. James Branch Cabell. New Haven, Connecticut: College and University Press, 174 pp.

This is an extended critical study, presenting the most nearly complete biographical data to date, along with analyses of Cabell's works.

3 WELLS, ARVIN. Jesting Moses: A Study in Cabellian Comedy. Gainesville: University of Florida Press, 146 pp.
The author devotes most of his attention to the Biography of Manuel in which he finds that Cabell "elaborated a point of view which is unique at least in American literature, and developed a distinctive literary technique as a means of expressing his view."

1962 B SHORTER WRITINGS

1 ANON. Review of Between Friends. Kirkus Reviews, 30 (15 February), 205.
The letters are "in fact period piece curiosa, a nostalgic entertainment for old guard literati...and slim pickings for anyone else."

2 ANON. "Greatest Since Hawthorne." Richmond Times-Dispatch (19 April), p. 12.
The author provides an editorial tribute to Cabell upon the occasion of the publication of Between Friends.

3 ANON. Review of Between Friends. New Yorker, 38 (21 April), 183-184.
Although these letters are important, they chronicle the works and lives of has-been writers.

4 CREEKMORE, HUBERT. "In the Twenties." New York Times Book Review (13 May), p. 5.
After recounting Cabell's rise and fall in popularity, the reviewer praises the thorough job of editing on Between Friends.

5 DURHAM, FRANK. "The Author Who Died Twice." The Georgia Review, 16 (Summer), 162-168.
The author offers an appraisal of Cabell's works four years after his death. (This essay was originally presented orally over the national network, Australian Broadcasting Commission.)

6 FERGUSON, DeLANCEY. "After 'Jurgen.'" New York Herald Tribune Books (15 April), p. 11.
The reviewer praises the "superb editing" done on Between Friends.

1962

7 GRAY, JAMES. Review of Between Friends. Saturday Review of Literature, 45 (5 May), 22.
After briefly surveying the Cabell era, the reviewer finds the letters to be dated. He concludes that even "old Cabell admirers are likely to wonder if Cabell has not already had his due."

8 HERZBERG, MAX J. "James Branch Cabell," in his The Reader's Encyclopedia of American Literature. New York: Thomas Y. Crowell, pp. 131-132.
The author provides a brief statement about Cabell, his fictional world, his work, and his reputation.

*9 HOFMAN, VON. Wayward Mother. Fabian Books, passim.
This novel contains various references to Cabell. Unlocatable, cited in Hall, 1974.A1.

10 PALLETTE, D. B. Review of Between Friends. The Arizona Quarterly, 18 (Winter), 375-376.
After commenting on Cabell's literary rise and fall, the reviewer notes that "literary historians will find this volume of value."

11 PETERS, EMMET, JR. "Cabell: The Making of a Rebel." The Carolina Quarterly, 14 (Spring), 74-81.
The author explores a homosexual incident at the College of William and Mary and a Richmond murder, both of which allegedly involved Cabell, finding that these events caused Cabell to withdraw from Richmond society.

12 ROUSE, BLAIR. Ellen Glasgow. New Haven, Connecticut: College and University Press, 160 pp., passim.
There are numerous references to Cabell throughout this book.

13 STEELE, OLIVER R. "Half-Sheet Imposition of Eight-Leaf Quires in Formes of Thirty-two and Sixty-four Pages." Studies in Bibliography, 15 (1962), 274-278.
A study of printing methods.

14 WAGENKNECHT, EDWARD. "An Author and his Correspondents." Chicago Sunday Tribune Magazine of Books (1 April), p. 2.
"This is an utterly charming and delightful book."

1963 A BOOKS--NONE

1963 B SHORTER WRITINGS

1 FISHER, VARDIS. Thomas Wolfe As I Knew Him and Other Essays. Denver, Colorado: Alan Swallow, passim.
There are minor references to Cabell in these collected essays.

2 HORAN, THOMAS. "Tea Party at Poynton Lodge." The Arthur Machen Journal, 1 (Summer), 26-29.
The author provides a report of a visit with Cabell in which he comments on Cabell's library and his prose style.

*3 PIPER, H. BEAM. The Cosmic Computer. New York: Ace Books.
This novel makes dramatic use of Cabellian names and places. Unlocatable, cited in Hall, 1974.A1.

4 ROUSE, BLAIR. Review of Between Friends. American Literature, 34 (January), 586-588.
The reviewer summarizes the book, noting that Jurgen was helpful in the battle against censorship.

5 SCHWAB, ARNOLD T. James Gibbons Huneker. Stanford, California: Stanford University Press, pp. 270-273.
The author provides passing comments on Cabell, linking him to the other writers of his day.

6 STEVENSON, SAMUEL W. "James Branch Cabell: Literary Master." Richmond Times-Dispatch (10 February), L, pp. 1, 7.
The author provides an overview of Cabell, his works, and the era in which he wrote.

7 STEVENSON, SAMUEL W. "'Jurgen' Was Center of a Storm." Richmond Times-Dispatch (17 February), L, pp. 1, 7.
The author retells the story of the trial of Jurgen.

8 STEVENSON, SAMUEL W. "Cabell Invented an Ideal Locale for His Writing." Richmond Times-Dispatch (24 February), L, pp. 1, 4.
The author describes Cabell's mythical realm of Poictesme.

9 STEVENSON, SAMUEL W. "'The Biography' by Cabell Covers Several Generations." Richmond Times-Dispatch (3 March), L, pp. 1, 3.
The author provides a discussion of the Biography of Manuel.

10 TOKLAS, ALICE B. What is Remembered. Chicago: Holt, Rinehart and Winston, p. 150.

1964

Miss Toklas reports Cabell's remarks about Gertrude Stein at a dinner in Richmond: "At dinner I sat next to James Branch Cabell who asked me, 'Is Gertrude Stein Serious?' 'Desperately,' I replied. 'That puts a different light on it,' he said. 'For you,' I said, 'not for me.'" (This is the entire quotation regarding Cabell.)

1964 A BOOKS--NONE

1964 B SHORTER WRITINGS

1 DURHAM, FRANK. "Love as a Literary Exercise: Young James Branch Cabell Tries His Wings." The Mississippi Quarterly, 18 (Winter), 26-37.
The author quotes from and discusses a series of letters between Cabell and Miss Norvell Harrison written when the former was a reporter in New York City, at the outset of his writing career.

2 KELLY, WILLIAM W. Ellen Glasgow: A Bibliography. Charlottesville: The Bibliographical Society of the University of Virginia, University Press of Virginia, passim.
Because Cabell and Miss Glasgow were close literary and personal friends, this book contains myriad references to him and his works.

3 McCOLLUM, N. M. "Glasgow's and Cabell's Comedies of Virginia." The Georgia Review, 18 (Summer), 236-241.
In a number of their novels, James Branch Cabell and Ellen Glasgow wrote of "the prolonged worship of chivalric traditions" during the late nineteenth and early twentieth century in Virginia.

4 NOLTE, WILLIAM H. H. L. Mencken: Literary Critic. Middletown, Connecticut: Wesleyan University Press, passim.
References to Cabell appear on twelve pages of this book.

5 QUINN, ARTHUR HOBSON. "Booth Tarkington and the Later Romance," in his American Fiction. New York: D. Appleton-Century, pp. 608-615.
Reprint of 1936.B9.

6 SCHLEGEL, DOROTHY. "James Branch Cabell and Southern Romanticism," in Southern Writers: Appraisals in Our Time. Edited by R. C. Simonini. Charlottesville: University Press of Virginia, pp. 124-141.
Reprint of 1959.B3; and reprinted 1975.A5.

1965 A BOOKS--NONE

1965 B SHORTER WRITINGS

1 CANARY, ROBERT. "James Branch Cabell and the Comedy of Skeptical Conservatism." Midcontinent American Studies Journal, 6 (Spring), 52-60.
The author provides a reappraisal of Cabell's works in light of the mid 1960s, asserting that the "fictional universe of Cabell's novels suggests a skepticism which can see through bourgeois ideals but cannot see beyond them."

2 CLARK, EMILY. Ingenue Among the Lions: The Letters of Emily Clark to Joseph Hergesheimer. Edited by Gerald Langford. Austin: University of Texas Press, passim.
These letters, often cattishly written, by the editor of The Reviewer, contain myriad references to Cabell, his family, and Richmond life and letters of the 1920s.

3 EDGAR, PELHAM. "Two Anti-Realists: Willa Cather and Cabell," in his The Art of the Novel: From 1700 to the Present Time. New York: Russell and Russell, pp. 261-267. Reprint of 1933.B3.

4 HALL, JAMES N. "Mundus Vult Decipi: An Uncritical Evaluation of James Branch Cabell." Kalki, I, No. 1, 4-5.
The author notes his amazement that Cabell's name is not usually listed among the great fantasy writers.

5 HALL, JAMES N. "The Biography of Manuel: A Brief Bibliography." Kalki, I, No. 2 (November), 12-14.
The author lists various volumes in various editions of the Biography of Manuel in the order in which they should be read, rather than the order in which they were written.

6 HOUSTON, CHARLES ["MIKE"]. "Old 'Jurgen' Back on Visit." Richmond News Leader (11 March), p. 17.
The author provides biographical notes on Cabell, occasioned by the presentation of a bust of Cabell to the Richmond Public Library by the Friends of the Library.

7 JOHNSON, MERLE. Merle Johnson's American First Editions. Fourth Edition. Edited by Jacob Blanck. Waltham, Massachusetts: Mark Press, pp. 87-91.
Revision and reprint of 1942.B8.

1965

8 WILSON, EDMUND. "James Branch Cabell: 1879-1958," in his The Bit Between My Teeth: A Literary Chronicle of 1950-65. New York: Farrar, Straus.
Reprint of 1958.B8.

1966 A BOOKS--NONE

1966 B SHORTER WRITINGS

1 DOLMETCH, CARL R. The Smart Set: A History and Anthology. New York: Dial Press, pp. 258-262.
In discussing Cabell's contributions to the magazine, the author finds that he "was Smart Set 'cleverness' incarnate."

2 DUGGAN, FRANCIS X. Paul Elmer More. New Haven, Connecticut: College and University Press, pp. 124-125.
The author comments that More thought Cabell's fame was "Owing chiefly to the postal authorities," and that he himself was "superficial," "sophisticated" and "snobbish."

1967 A BOOKS

1 TARRANT, DESMOND. James Branch Cabell: The Dream and the Reality. Norman: University of Oklahoma Press, 292 pp.
The author provides a study of Cabell's dramatic vision and artistry as it permeates his entire canon.

1967 B SHORTER WRITINGS

1 BLISH, JAMES. "Nizian Gets One Right." Kalki, 2, No. 1, 2.
Chapter 54 of The Silver Stallion has its origin in an "authentic ritual of black magic derived from the Grand Grimoire of Antonio Venitiana del Rabina" published circa 1750.

2 BLISH, JAMES. "Birdsong." Kalki, 2, No. 1, 5.
Figures of Earth Cabell uses historically accurate nonsense words "by which medieval poets verbalized the song of the nightingale."

3 BLISH, JAMES. "At the Altar of Sesphra: An Approach to the Allegory." Kalki, 2, No. 1, 6-7, 17.
"The Biography of the Life of Manuel is full of exotic names..., many of which contain hidden meanings of various

sorts, which serve as an important guide to Cabell's often obviously allegorical intent."

4 BLISH, JAMES. "The Anagram Game: More About Mother and Elsewhere." Kalki, 2, No. 1, 17.
The author finds the probable anagrams in Cabell's Serda and Antan.

5 BLISH, JAMES. "A Horrible Quiet Noise." Kalki, 2, No. 2, 26.
The source for Chapter 25 of The Cream of the Jest is in Roger Bacon's communication about gunpowder to Pope Clement IV in 1265.

6 BLISH, JAMES. "The Anagram Game: Three More." Kalki, 2, No. 2, 39.
The author finds anagrams for Cabell's Horvendile, Anaïtis, and Porutsa.

7 BLISH, JAMES. "To Rhadamanthus Snarling: Cabell Against His Critics." Kalki, 2, No. 3, 43-47.
The author traces Cabell's published attacks upon his detractors.

8 BLISH, JAMES. "The Problem of Scoteia." Kalki, 2, No. 3, 48-49.
The author attempts to find an anagram for Cabell's Scoteia.

9 BLISH, JAMES. "Ettarre an Anagram?" Kalki, 2, No. 3, 49.
There is a possibility that Ettarre is an anagram for "retreat" and/or "theater."

10 BLISH, JAMES. "The Jurgen Suite." Kalki, 2, No. 3, 61.
The author notes that a recording company, possibly Decca, recorded Deems Taylor's symphonic poem "Jurgen."

11 BLISH, JAMES. "Source Notes: More Spells." Kalki, 2, No. 3, 62-63.
The author finds authentic rituals of black magic in The Silver Stallion and Something About Eve.

12 BLISH, JAMES. "Some Cabellian Tropes." Kalki, 2, No. 3, 66-67.
The author provides assorted notes on Cabell's use of tropes.

13 GODSHALK, WILLIAM LEIGH. "James Branch Cabell at William and Mary: The Education of a Novelist." William and Mary Review, 5, No. 2, 1-10. Reprint 1975.A3.

The author discusses Cabell's performance as a student along with the alleged homosexual episode during his college days.

14 HALL, JAMES N. "The Biography of Manuel: A Brief Bibliography." Kalki, 2, No. 1, 3-5.
The author lists various volumes in various editions of the Biography of Manuel in the order in which they should be read, rather than the order in which they were written.

15 HALL, JAMES N. "The Re-Evolution of a Vestryman: A Study in Cabellian Theology." Kalki, 2, No. 4a, 72-76.
The author finds that Cabell's religious views changed during "the period when he went from obscurity to the best-seller lists."

16 HALL, JAMES N. and PAUL SPENCER. "Source Notes: The Silver Stallion." Kalki, 2, No. 1, 17.
"Kalki in Hindu mythology is the name of the tenth incarnation of Vishnu, which is yet to come."

17 JAMES, EDWARD M. "Palatoki." Kalki, 2, No. 1, 16.
The author traces The Silver Stallion to the Danish Eyrbggja saga as popularized by E. R. Eddison.

18 MENCKEN, H. L. "Cabell Major," in James Branch Cabell: Three Essays by Carl Van Doren, H. L. Mencken, and Hugh Walpole. No editor listed. Port Washington, New York: Kennikat Press, pp. 31-57.
Reprint of 1927.A1.

19 RUBIN, LOUIS D., JR. "Two in Richmond: Ellen Glasgow and James Branch Cabell," in his The Curious Death of the Novel. Baton Rouge: Louisiana State University Press, pp. 152-182.
Reprint of 1961.B3.

20 RULAND, RICHARD. "H. L. Mencken," in his The Rediscovery of American Literature. Cambridge, Massachusetts: Harvard University Press, passim.
In a discussion of H. L. Mencken, the author makes passing references to Cabell.

21 SPENCER, PAUL. "A Manual of Non-Manuals: A Further Bibliography." Kalki, 2, No. 2, 29-31.
The author provides a list of the post-Biography books centering on the life of Manuel.

22 VAN DOREN, CARL. "Cabell Minor," in James Branch Cabell: Three Essays by Carl Van Doren, H. L. Mencken, and Hugh Walpole. No editor listed. Port Washington, New York: Kennikat Press, pp. 1-30.
Reprint of 1925.A2.

23 WALPOLE, HUGH. "Scholia," in James Branch Cabell: Three Essays by Carl Van Doren, H. L. Mencken, and Hugh Walpole. No editor listed. Port Washington, New York: Kennikat Press, pp. 58-86.
Reprint of 1920.A2.

1968 A BOOKS--NONE

1968 B SHORTER WRITINGS

1 BEACH, JOSEPH WARREN. "James Branch Cabell," in his The Outlook for American Prose. Freeport, New York: Books for Libraries Press, pp. 63-80.
Reprint of 1926.B12.

2 BOYER, PAUL S. Purity in Print. New York: Charles Scribner's Sons, passim.
The author makes numerous passing references to the trial of Jurgen.

3 BRUSSEL, I. R. "The First Fifty Years of Jurgen." The Cabellian, 1, No. 2, 74.
The author provides a short note on the publishing history of Jurgen.

4 CANARY, ROBERT H. "Cabell's Dark Comedies." The Mississippi Quarterly, 21 (Spring), 83-92.
Using a psychoanalytic viewpoint to explore Cabell's treatment of sex, the author finds that Cabell's "sexual comedy resembles Shakespeare's Measure for Measure more than it does As You Like It."

5 DAVIS, JOE LEE. "Recent Cabell Criticism." The Cabellian, 1, No. 1, 1-12.
The author provides a summary of the contemporary attitudes about Cabell's works.

6 DUKE, MAURICE. "James Branch Cabell's Personal Library: A Summary." The Cabellian, 1, No. 1, 27-30.

The author provides brief comments about Cabell's personal books and the way he kept, annotated, and cared for them. Revised and enlarged 1970.B8.

7 JAMES, EDWARD M. "Cabellian Economics: The Uses of the Short Stories." Kalki, 2, No. 4a, 101-102.
The author provides comments on Cabell's reuse of his materials.

8 KELLNER, BRUCE. Carl Van Vechten and the Irreverent Decade. Norman: University of Oklahoma Press, 354 pp., passim.
There are references to Cabell on twenty-two separate pages of this book.

9 LAWRENCE, JUDITH ANN [MRS. JAMES BLISH]. "Poictesme." Kalki, 2, No. 4a, 87-88.
The artist provides a cartographic rendition of Cabell's Poictesme.

10 MacDONALD, EDGAR E. "Cabell Criticism: Past, Present, and Future." The Cabellian, 1, No. 1, 21-25.
The author provides an overview of critical attitudes about Cabell's works.

11 MacDONALD, EDGAR E. "The Storisende Edition: Some Liabilities." The Cabellian, 1, No. 2, 64-67.
The author considers the weak points of the Biography of Manuel as a unified work.

12 MAYFIELD, SARA. The Constant Circle: H. L. Mencken and His Friends. New York: Delacorte Press, 307 pp., passim.
There are references to Cabell on twenty-six separate pages of this book. They center on his works and his relationship with Emily Clark.

13 PARKS, EDD WINFIELD. "James Branch Cabell." The Mississippi Quarterly, 20 (Spring), 97-102.
The author provides an appraisal of Cabell's reputation, noting his strengths and his weaknesses.

14 PATTEE, FRED LEWIS. "James Branch Cabell," in his New American Literature, 1890-1930. New York: Century, pp. 350-355.
Reprint of 1930.B13.

15 REEVES, PASCHAL. "From Halley's Comet to Prohibition." The Mississippi Quarterly, 21 (Fall), 286-287.
Cabell is included here in a general discussion of Southern literature from 1910 to 1920.

16 ROTHMAN, JULIUS. "Jurgen, the Rabelaisian Babbitt." The Cabellian, 1, No. 1, 35-40.
The author points out that the cosmic irony and burlesque in Jurgen are similar to that found in Rabelais.

17 SCHLEGEL, DOROTHY. "A Case of Literary Piracy?" The Cabellian, 1, No. 2, 58-63.
The author explores the controversy of Cabell's use of Edwin Dart Lambright's The Life and Exploits of Gasparilla in writing There Were Two Pirates. Reprinted 1975.A5.

1969 A BOOKS--NONE

1969 B SHORTER WRITINGS

1 ADLER, BETTY, comp. Man of Letters: A Census of the Correspondence of H. L. Mencken. Baltimore, Maryland: Enoch Pratt Free Library.
This census locates 404 letters from Cabell to Mencken covering the period from 1919 to 1951.

2 ANDERSON, POUL. "Something About the Gods." Kalki, 3, No. 1, 20-21.
The author provides notes on Cabell's use of Old Scandinavian mythology in The Silver Stallion.

3 BLISH, JAMES. "Cabell as Kabbalist." Kalki, 3, No. 2, 11-12.
The author provides notes on the history of the word "demiurge."

4 BLISH, JAMES. "The Tolkien of the Twenties Returns." Chicago Tribune Book World (6 July), p. 8.
The author provides an article on the current Cabell revival.

5 BLISH, JAMES. "Cabell as Voluntarist." Kalki, 3, No. 4 (Fall), 120-122.
The author finds that Cabell subscribed to the nineteenth century school of philosophy known as Voluntarism.

6 BLISH, JAMES. "Did Cabell Use the Tarot Deck?" Kalki, 3, No. 4 (Fall), 145-146.
Cabell may have used the Tarot cards in several of his novels.

1969

7 BLISH, JAMES and JAMES N. HALL. "Cabell as Historical Actor." Kalki, 3, No. 2, 43-45.
Contrary to what is usually believed, Cabell was involved in the activities of the world around him.

8 BOARDMAN, JOHN. "The Two Cabells." Kalki, 3, No. 3 (Summer), 83-85.
The author finds that Cabell created his surrogate as Horvendile in his novels.

9 BODE, CARL. Mencken. Carbondale: Southern Illinois University Press, 452 pp., passim.
This biography contains a number of references to Cabell.

10 CANARY, ROBERT H. "Cabelliana in Hawaii." The Cabellian, 2, No. 1, 27.
The author comments upon five letters from Cabell to A. Grove Day, author of the unpublished "Cabell: A Comedy of Interpretation."

11 CARTER, LIN. "Horvendile--A Link Between Cabell and Tolkien." Kalki, 3, No. 3 (Summer), 85-87.
In his book Tolkien: A Look Behind "The Lord of the Rings" (New York: Ballentine, 1969), Carter has a good deal of material pertinent to Cabell.

12 DUKE, MAURICE. "Sinclair Lewis on the Highway: An Unpublished Letter." The Sinclair Lewis Newsletter, 1 (Spring), 2.
The author edits and publishes a letter from Lewis to Cabell recounting the problems incurred when the former visited the latter in Rockbridge Alum Springs, Virginia.

13 FLORA, JOSEPH M. "Vardis Fisher and James Branch Cabell: An Essay on Influence and Reputation." The Cabellian, 2, No. 1, 12-16.
The author finds that Cabell had great influence on Fisher and hence "Cabell is one of our great realists."

14 GABBARD, G. M. "Now About The Silver Stallion." Kalki, 3, No. 1, 33.
The author provides notes on Cabell's sources for the book.

15 GABBARD, G. N. "More About Sylans." Kalki, 3, No. 2 (Spring), 69.
The author finds the probable origin of Sylan, a word often used by Cabell.

16 GABBARD, G. N. "Flamberge." Kalki, 3, No. 2 (Spring), 74.
The author finds a definition of "Flamberge," a word used by Cabell, in Stone's Glossary of Arms and Armor.

17 HALPER, NATHAN. "Joyce and James Branch Cabell." A Wake Newsletter, 6 (August), 51-60. Published by the Department of English, University of Dundee, Scotland.
Citing evidence from James Joyce's Finnegans Wake, the author suggests the possibility of Cabell's having influenced his writing of that book. See following entry.

18 HALPER, NATHAN. "Joyce/Cabell and Cabell/Joyce." Kalki, 4, No. 1 (Winter), 9-24.
Revision and reprint of 1969.B17.

19 INGE, M. THOMAS. "The Unheeding South: Donald Davidson on James Branch Cabell." The Cabellian, 2, No. 1, 17-20.
The author reprints and comments upon a negative review of Something About Eve written by Donald Davidson.

20 JENKINS, WILLIAM D. "The Shirt of Nessus." Kalki, 3, No. 1, 9-10.
The use of the classical allusion in Jurgen, the author finds, indicates that Jurgen wears his monogamy lightly.

21 JENKINS, WILLIAM D. "Alcluid Unclouded." Kalki, 3, No. 2 (Spring), 10.
The author finds that Cabell's fictional Alcluid is a blend of the Celtic Alcluith and Alclyde.

22 JENKINS, WILLIAM D. "A Time for Airy Persiflage." Kalki, 3, No. 2 (Spring), 50-52.
The author finds that Cabell sometimes echoes Gilbert and Sullivan's The Mikado.

23 JENKINS, WILLIAM D. "Another Way of Elusion." Kalki, 3, No. 2 (Spring), 63-69.
The author provides notes on Cabell's literary sources.

24 JENKINS, WILLIAM D. "Our Lady of Pain; or, Sundry Devices of the Philistines." Kalki, 4, No. 1 (Winter), 25-26.
The author finds that Cabell borrowed the tumble-bug, or dung-beetle, as the enemy of art from Swinburne.

25 JOHNSON, MERLE. Merle Johnson's American First Editions. Fourth Edition. Edited by Jacob Blanck. Waltham, Massachusetts: Mark Press, pp. 87-91.
Reprint of 1965.B7.

1969

26 MacDONALD, EDGAR E. "The Glasgow-Cabell Entente." American Literature, 41 (March), 76-91.
The author explores the delicate relationship between the two Richmond writers, who often were subtly out of favor with each other.

27 MacDONALD, EDGAR E. "Cabell's Hero: Cosmic Rebel." The Southern Literary Journal, 2 (Fall), 22-42.
The author provides a detailed study of the man and the writer, seeing his canon as representing one central character in rebellion against the universe.

28 PETER, EMMETT, JR. "Another Mirror for Pigeons." Kalki, 3, No. 3 (Summer), 88-91.
The author finds that the mirror and the pigeon are two of Cabell's most often used symbols.

29 SCHLEGEL, DOROTHY B. "James Branch Cabell," in A Bibliographical Guide to the Study of Southern Literature. Edited by Louis D. Rubin, Jr. Baton Rouge, Louisiana: Louisiana State University Press, pp. 163-165.
The compiler lists the major secondary sources applicable to a study of Cabell.

30 SCHLEGEL, DOROTHY B. "Cabell's Translation of Virginia." The Cabellian, 2, No. 1 (Autumn), 1-11.
The author comments upon the various ways in which Cabell dramatized the state of Virginia in his works. Reprinted 1975.A5.

31 SCHLEGEL, DOROTHY B. "James Branch Cabell: A Latter-Day Enlightener." College Language Association Journal, 12 (March), 223-236.
The author finds that Cabell's religious views resemble those of the eighteenth century Enlighteners, especially the French ones. Reprinted 1975.A5.

32 SMITH, NELSON J., III. "Cabell: Realist or Romantic?" Kalki, 3, No. 2 (Spring), 53-56.
"Cabell is a supreme realist who faced unflinchingly what he saw to be the facts of human experience."

33 SPENCER, PAUL. "After the Style of Maurice Hewlett." Kalki, 3, No. 4 (Fall), 143-145.
The author discusses the possible influence of Hewlett on Cabell.

34 STAPLES, ROGER. "The Lance and the Veil." Kalki, 4, No. 1 (Winter), 3-8.
The author finds that Cabell relied on Aleister Crowley and the Gnostic Mass for parts of Jurgen.

35 ZIRKLE, CONWAY. "Cabell and Wilson." Kalki, 3, No. 2 (Spring), 46-49.
"Cabell's evaluation of Woodrow Wilson underwent a complete reversal between 1916 and 1919."

36 ZIRKLE, CONWAY. "The Anagram Game." Kalki, 3, No. 3 (Summer), 103.
The author identifies three more anagrams in Figures of Earth.

1970 A BOOKS

1 UNTERMEYER, LOUIS. "James Branch Cabell: The Man and His Masks." Richmond, Virginia: The Associates of the James Branch Cabell Library, 21 pp.
This pamphlet is a general appraisal of Cabell and his works by an old friend and admirer.

1970 B SHORTER WRITINGS

1 ADLER, BETTY. "The Mencken Room." The Cabellian, 3, No. 1 (Autumn), 28-30.
The author notes how Mencken's friendship with Cabell is manifest in the Mencken Room of the Enoch Pratt Free Library in Baltimore, Maryland.

2 ALLAN, JAMES. "Cabell and Mac Donald [sic]." Kalki, 4, No. 4, 138-142.
The author finds that Cabell was probably influenced by George Macdonald [sic].

3 BLISH, JAMES. "The Stallion's Other Members." Kalki, 4, No. 2, 67-69.
The author finds that The Silver Stallion has a problematical and complex structure.

4 BLISH, JAMES. "The Geography of Dream." Kalki, 4, No. 3, 90-92.
Cabell extended the geographical boundaries of Poictesme after completing the Biography of Manuel.

1970

5 CANARY, ROBERT H. "Fables of Art in The Silver Stallion." Kalki, 4, No. 2, 42-44.
"Cabell's self-creating heroes embody the experience of 'the whole human race.'"

6 CARSON, BETTY FARLEY. "Richmond Renascence: The Virginia Writers' Club of the 1920's and The Reviewer." The Cabellian, 2, No. 2 (Spring), 39-47.
The author provides a history of the club, including Cabell's relationship to it.

7 DAVIS, RICHARD BEALE, C. HUGH HOLMAN and LOUIS D. RUBIN, JR. Southern Writing: 1588-1920. New York: Odyssey Press, pp. 953-954.
In this anthology Cabell is briefly introduced, with the conclusion that "there is reason to think that he will continue to have his admirers and to be read and enjoyed for decades to come."

8 DUKE, MAURICE. "James Branch Cabell's Personal Library." Studies in Bibliography, 23: 207-216.
Revised and enlarged version of 1968.B6.

9 EARNEST, ERNEST. The Single Vision: The Alienation of American Intellectuals, 1910-1930. New York: New York University Press, 241 pp.
Includes several references to Cabell.

10 FLORA, JOSEPH M. "The Structure of The Silver Stallion." Kalki, 4, No. 2, 38-41.
The episodes in the book, the author finds, provide great variety...and emphasize the great skill of their creator.

11 FLORA, JOSEPH M. "Vardis Fisher and James Branch Cabell: A Postscript." The Cabellian, 3, No. 1 (Autumn), 7-9.
The author notes ways in which Fisher made literary use of Cabell.

12 GABBARD, G. N. "Deems Taylor's Musical Version of Jurgen." The Cabellian, 3, No. 1 (Autumn), 12-15.
The author reproduces the New York Times' notices and reviews of Taylor's Jurgen.

13 GABBARD, G. N. "Fairy Tales in The High Place." Kalki, 4, No. 4, 115-120.
Cabell's The High Place is "the usual fairy story, pursued beyond its conventional ending."

1970

14 HENSLEY, DONALD M. Burton Rascoe. New Haven, Connecticut: College and University Press, 162 pp., passim.
This book contains myriad references to Cabell.

15 JENKINS, WILLIAM D. "The Cabell Arms." Kalki, 4, No. 2, 34, 75.
The author provides notes on Cabell's coat of arms.

16 MacDONALD, EDGAR E. "Cabell's Richmond Trial." The Southern Literary Journal, 3 (Fall), 47-71.
The author finds references in numerous books by Cabell to the John Scott murder case, in which Cabell was allegedly involved. The author also refers to Cabell's having left the College of William and Mary under a cloud of homosexual controversy.

17 MacDONALD, EDGAR E. "The Influence of Provençal Poetry on James Branch Cabell." The Cabellian, 3, No. 1, 1-6.
The author discusses Cabell's relationship to the works of the Provençal poets.

18 MILLETT, FRED B. "James Branch Cabell," in Minor American Authors. Edited by Charles A. Hoyt. Carbondale: Southern Illinois University Press, 140 pp.
See the preface to this book for a derogatory view of Cabell.

19 PARKINSON, BOB. "Eschatologies of Manuel." Kalki, 4, No. 2, 70-71.
The author discusses the structure of The Silver Stallion.

20 SPENCER, PAUL. "Coth and Tohueyo." Kalki, 4, No. 2, 72, 74.
The author finds that many details in The Silver Stallion "have striking parallels in Mexican legendry."

21 TARRANT, DESMOND. "Cabell's Hamlet Had an Uncle and Shakespeare's Hamlet." The Cabellian, 3, No. 1 (Autumn), 10-11.
The author provides a short article on the similarity between Cabell's and Shakespeare's Hamlets, noting that the more profound symbolic version is Cabell's.

22 TARRANT, DESMOND. "Stallion and Legend." Kalki, 4, No. 2, 64-66.
The Silver Stallion "thrashes out in fiction the arguments which, ultimately, are in support of faith, however dubious its origins and reasons."

1970

23 WELCH, EMMONS. "Beyond Life and Jurgen: The Demiurge." The Cabellian, 2, No. 2 (Spring), 48-53.
The writer examines the two novels "in light of Cabell's philosophical perspective."

24 ZIRKLE, CONWAY. "Circular Time Travel." Kalki, 4, No. 3, 84-87.
The author finds that many of Cabell's fictional characters travel in a loop of time, beginning where they end.

1971 A BOOKS

1 BREWER, FRANCES JOAN. James Branch Cabell: A Bibliography of His Writings, Biography and Criticism. Freeport, New York: Books for Libraries, 206 pp.
Reprint of 1957.A1.

1971 B SHORTER WRITINGS

1 BLISH, JAMES. "Cabell as a Playright." Kalki, 5, No. 2, 35-37.
Cabell's only play, The Jewel Merchants, would act easily and "would make a splendid radio or TV play."

2 CHURCHILL, ALLEN. The Literary Decade. New York: Prentice Hall, pp. 51-55 and passim.
The author views Cabell and his works in retrospect, concluding that "Today, fifty years later," Cabell and others like him, "once marked for immortality are little more than footnotes in our cultural history."

*3 COLLETON, JOHN. The Trembling of a Leaf. New York: Pocket Books.
This novel has favorable references to Cabell in it. Unlocatable, cited in Hall, 1974.A1.

4 DUKE, MAURICE. "The Reviewer: A Bibliographical Guide to a Little Magazine." Resources for American Literary Study, 1 (Spring), 58-103.
The compiler provides an annotated list of the contents of The Reviewer, edited briefly by Cabell, along with scattered comments about him.

5 GABBARD, G. N. "Jurgen and Peer Gynt." Kalki, 5, No. 1, 3-4.
"Some influence from Ibsen seems to be visible in Jurgen."

6 LUNDWALL, SAM J. Science Fiction: What It's All About. New York: Ace Books, pp. 98-101.
In a brief discussion of Cabell's works, the author finds that "Cabell is at bottom disillusioned, and his humor... underlines this."

7 MacDONALD, EDGAR E. "Cabell's Game of Hide and Seek." The Cabellian, 4, No. 1 (Autumn), 9-16.
The author comments on and investigates Cabell's success at making the Biography of Manuel a unified work.

8 McNEILL, WARREN A. "James Branch Cabell 'In Time's Hourglass.'" The Cabellian, 3, No. 2 (Spring), 64-70.
The author reports on several personal meetings with Cabell.

9 MORLEY-MOWER, GEOFFREY. "Cabell's Reputation and Jurgen." Kalki, 5, No. 1, 24-29.
The author finds that Cabell is well equipped to debunk the Playboy solutions to life. Reprinted 1975.B4.

10 SCHLEGEL, DOROTHY B. "Cabell and His Critics." The Cabellian, 3, No. 2 (Spring), 50-63.
The author explores Cabell's relationship to his critics. Revision and reprint of 1961.B4; and reprinted 1975.A5.

11 SCHLEGEL, DOROTHY B. "Cabell's Comic Mask." The Cabellian, 4, No. 1 (Autumn), 1-8.
The author argues that in his writings Cabell dons "the mask of comedy to hide his heartache and despair."

12 SIEGLE, LIN C. "Dating in Figures of Earth." The Cabellian, 4, No. 1 (Autumn), 17-21.
In Figures of Earth Cabell employs festivals and celebrations to define temporally the "multi-faceted identity of Manuel...."

13 YOCUM, JOANNE. "The Triumph of Romantic Realism." Kalki, 5, No. 3, 85-92.
The author finds that all the lords in The Silver Stallion were made into "true children of the spirit of Manuel," by Romantic idealism.

1972 A BOOKS--NONE

1972

1972 B SHORTER WRITINGS

1 BLISH, JAMES. "The Long Night of a Virginia Author." The Journal of Modern Literature, 2: 393-405.

In a detailed critical reading of The Nightmare Has Triplets, the author finds that the trilogy "stands at the heart" of Cabell's later work.

2 BUFORD, ROB. "The Life of James Branch Cabell." Richmond Mercury Book Review (6 December), pp. 1, 14-15.

The author provides a general article about Cabell and his literary reputation.

3 CHESLOCK, LOUIS. "The Jewel Merchants, an Opera: A Case History." The Cabellian, 4, No. 2 (Spring), 68-84.

Drawing on an assortment of letters, the author chronicles the history of the play.

4 DAVIS, JOE LEE. "Cabell and Santayana in the Neo-Humanist Debate." The Cabellian, 4, No. 2 (Spring), 55-67.

The author discusses the reactions of Cabell and Santayana to the New Humanists.

5 DUKE, MAURICE. "Letters of George Sterling to James Branch Cabell." American Literature, 44 (March), 146-153.

These edited letters chronicle the brief and abortive friendship between the two writers.

6 HUBBELL, JAY B. Who Are the Major American Writers? Durham, North Carolina: Duke University Press, passim.

The author mentions Cabell and his books in a number of places.

7 MORLEY-MOWER, GEOFFREY F. "James Branch Cabell's Flirtation with Clio: The Story of a Collaboration." Yale University Library Gazette, 47 (July), 15-27.

The author explores and explains the ways in which Cabell and A. J. Hanna jointly wrote The St. Johns. Reprinted 1975.B4.

8 TAYLOR, WELFORD DUNAWAY. "James Branch Cabell," in his Virginia Authors: Past and Present. Farmville, Virginia: Virginia Association of Teachers of English, pp. 20-21.

The author provides a short biographical entry, with a selected listing of secondary sources, on Cabell.

1973 A BOOKS--NONE

1973 B SHORTER WRITINGS

1 GODSHALK, WILLIAM LEIGH. "Cabell and Barth: Our Comic Athletes," in The Comic Imagination in American Literature. Edited by Louis D. Rubin, Jr. New Brunswick, New Jersey: Rutgers University Press, pp. 275-283.
The author finds that Cabell's "'resolute frivolity' and Barth's 'cheerful Nihilism' point to a similarity in artistic approach as well as a similarity in attitude." Reprint 1975.A3.

2 GODSHALK, WILLIAM LEIGH. "Cabell's Cream of the Jest and recent American fiction." The Southern Literary Journal, 5 (Spring), 18-31.
"In Cabell...we find a good deal that looks forward to the fiction of the last two decades."

1974 A BOOKS

1 HALL, JAMES N. James Branch Cabell: A Complete Bibliography. New York: Revisionist Press, 245 pp.
The compiler records all states, impressions, and editions of Cabell's works; his contributions to periodicals; and secondary criticism.

2 HIMELICK, RAYMOND. James Branch Cabell and the Modern Temper. New York: Revisionist Press, 24 pp.
Reprint of 1948.B5; 1956.B3; 1959.B1.

1974 B SHORTER WRITINGS

1 DUKE, MAURICE. "Cabell's and Glasgow's Richmond: The Intellectual Background of the City." The Mississippi Quarterly, 27 (Fall), 375-391.
The author traces the history of reading, the theater, and writing in Richmond during the nineteenth century.

2 DUKE, MAURICE. "The Ornate Wasteland of James Branch Cabell." Kalki, 6, No. 3, 79-89.
This article, published without the author's knowledge or authorization, finds that Cabell's world view, as dramatized in the Biography of Manuel, is similar to T. S. Eliot's, as found in The Waste Land. This is the unauthorized publication of 1975.B1.

1974

3 GODSHALK, WILLIAM LEIGH. "Cabell's Mirrors and (Incidentally) Pigeons." Kalki, 6, No. 2, 63-67.
Cabell's mirrors "are complex symbols...and each must be examined in the immediate context of the narrative." Reprint 1975.A3.

4 HOBSON, FRED C., JR. Serpent in Eden: H. L. Mencken and the South. Chapel Hill: University of North Carolina Press, passim.
The author makes references to Cabell throughout this book.

5 TARRANT, DESMOND. "On Visiting the Master." Kalki, 6, No. 3, 90-93.
The author reports on a visit to Cabell. Reprint 1975.A4.

1975 A BOOKS

1 BREGENZER, DON. A Round-Table in Poictesme. New York: Revisionist Press, 126 pp.
Reprint of 1924.A1.

*2 CANARY, ROBERT H. The Cabell Scene. New York: Revisionist Press.
Unseen.

3 GODSHALK, WILLIAM LEIGH. In Quest of Cabell. New York: Revisionist Press, 97 pp.
Reprint of 1967.B13; 1973.B1; 1974.B3; plus "The Growth of A Credo: Beyond Life," which traces Cabell's reworking of that novel; and "Selected Bibliography," which includes Secondary sources.

4 MORLEY-MOWER, GEOFFREY. Cabell Under Fire. New York: Revisionist Press, 29 pp.
Reprint of 1971.B9; 1972.B7; 1974.B5; plus "Cabell Under Fire," which retells the story of the suppression of Jurgen.

5 SCHLEGEL, DOROTHY B. James Branch Cabell: The Richmond Iconoclast. New York: Revisionist Press, 101 pp.
Reprint of 1964.B6; 1968.B17; 1969.B30, B31; 1971.B10.

6 WAGENKNECHT, EDWARD. The Letters of James Branch Cabell. Norman: University of Oklahoma Press, 277 pp.
The editor reproduces, with editorial comment, a number of Cabell's letters.

1975 B SHORTER WRITINGS

1 DUKE, MAURICE. "The Ornate Waste Land of James Branch Cabell," in The Twenties: Fiction, Poetry, Drama. Edited by Warren French. DeLand, Florida: Everett/Edwards, pp. 75-86.
See 1974.B2.

2 FLORA, JOSEPH M. "Cabell as Precursor: Reflections on Cabell and Vonnegut." Kalki, 6, No. 4, 118-137.
"Cabell prefigures Vonnegut."

3 KELLNER, BRUCE. "Alfred Kazin's Exquisites--An Excavation." The Illinois Quarterly, 38 (Fall), 45-62.
In discussing a chapter that Kazin deleted from later editions of On Native Grounds, the author makes numerous references to Cabell.

4 MEACHAM, HARRY. "Cabell's Letters Show His Brilliance." Richmond News Leader (26 February), p. 13.
With the publication of this book, "We now have a full-length portrait of one of the truly great writers of this century...."

5 MORLEY-MOWER, GEOFFREY. "Sinclair Lewis's Attempts to Reform James Branch Cabell." Kalki, 6, No. 4, 140-145.
When Lewis first read The Cream of the Jest he misunderstood it. Reprint of 1975.A4.

6 SCURA, DOROTHY. "Cabell's Personal Letters Illuminate the Author." Richmond Times-Dispatch (9 March), F, p. 5.
What emerges from these letters is "a portrait of the writer--totally committed, serious, concerned about every aspect of his work."

Index

Note: Only significant entries have been indexed.

Index